50 YEARS OF
SILENCE

Jan Ruff-O'Herne

Editions Tom Thompson
Sydney Amsterdam New York

Editions Tom Thompson
11 Cove Street, Watsons Bay, Sydney, NSW 2030, Australia

In association with
HarperCollins *Publishers*
25 Ryde Road, Pymble, Sydney, NSW 2073, Australia
31 View Road, Glenfield, Auckland 10, New Zealand
HarperCollins *International*
10 East 53rd Street, New York, NY 10022, USA

Distributed in the Netherlands by
Indeknipscheer
Uitgeverij, Singel 450, 1017 Av Amsterdam

First published in Australia in 1994

ISBN 1 875892 00 1

Cover photograph courtesy the author.
Designed by Robyn Latimer.
Printed in Australia by Griffin Press, Adelaide.

To my daughters Eileen and Carol

Acknowledgements

My thanks to Eileen and Garrie, Carol and Ned, Fien and
Céleste for encouraging me to write my story, and for all
their support. To my husband Tom, for his
understanding, and the O'Herne family, and Loeke and
Fröke, for all their love. To the Foundation of Japanese
Honorary Debts (Stichting Japanese Ereschulden),
especially Sjoerd Lapré, my thanks for their help and
inspiration. To Elizabeth Butel, who edited this book, and
publisher Tom Thompson.

To the first Korean 'comfort women' who had the courage
to speak out and gave me the courage to tell my story to
the world.

J. R-O.

The publisher would also like to acknowledge the help of
Ned Lander and Carol Ruff for access to images from
their documentary film *50 Years of Silence*.

Indonesian words and place names in this book have not
been modernised at the author's request.

Contents

Part 1

Each picture, a different story

'OMA, PLEASE tell me a story from when you were a little girl in Java?'

My little granddaughter was looking through my old photograph album. Her smiling face looked up at me in expectation.

'Which story do you want to hear this time?' I asked.

She turned the pages of the album carefully, almost with reverence, each picture, a different story.

'Tell me about the house, Oma, and about the little lizards climbing up the walls. Tell me about all the animals you had and the snake you caught, and when you fell out of the Banyan tree. Tell me about your French grandpa and how you always had to sit with a straight back at the table ... and what about when you went climbing the mountain and your legs got covered with black leeches. Tell me, tell me, Oma!'

I looked at the eager young face and I felt the urgency of passing on my story: the roots, the family traditions, the richness of the past. It was all there, buried among the pages of this family album.

There were some photographs which were absent, however, photographs which had never been taken. The images were deeply and permanently engraved on my mind and locked away in my heart, but the stories which they told had been kept secret because they were too shameful, too horrific to tell. I had kept them secret from my daughters, my grandchildren, from family and friends. The need to tell these darker stories was growing just as strong, just as powerful.

MY GRANDDAUGHTER had heard the beginning of the story, and the many small moments that made it up, so many times before. Like all children she loved repetition and the security of knowing what was coming next. I looked at the photos, some of them faded with age. Each picture held a treasured memory of a beautiful childhood spent in Java in the Netherlands East Indies, now called Indonesia.

I could feel again the heat and the humidity. I could hear the sounds of the distant gamelan music, mixed with the song of the cicadas and the crickets, filling the night with a tropical symphony. I could smell the mosquito coils burning as we sat on the front verandah of our house watching the toads jump up and down after the many insects. But most of all I remembered the smells — charcoal fires, tropical fruits, fragrant flowers, the unmistakable smell of the sate vendor.

Ours was a happy family and I had the most wonderful childhood anyone could imagine. I was the third of five children, growing up on a sugar factory plantation, called s.f. Tjepiering, near Semarang in central Java. My parents were loving, intelligent and artistic, both very talented in their own different way. I owe them so much. I am only what I am now because of my parents, who brought me up in the true

Catholic tradition, sending me to Catholic schools and college.

My parents, especially my father, implanted in me a great and strong faith and a love of prayer and Holy Scripture. This deep faith was my most precious gift from God, my support and my strength in the suffering that lay far in the future.

They were both musically gifted, with a great love of classical music. I have vivid memories of going to sleep at night listening to my parents making music together. My father was an excellent violinist, my mother an equally talented pianist and singer. She could sing in several languages but she had a preference for the Schubert lieder which she rendered most beautifully in her rich, mezzo-soprano voice.

My earliest memories of childhood go back to 1926, when I was three years old. My father was an amateur photographer and we had a darkroom on the back verandah. I was very stubborn as a child. One day I had wet my pants but insisted repeatedly that my older sister, Aline, had done it. My father was so shocked and infuriated by my persistent lie that he put me in this darkroom for punishment.

It was a harsh one for so young a child but fortunately I was not kept there for too long. I have never forgotten the experience of utter darkness, but it taught me the seriousness of telling a lie and the ugliness of it.

Another early, happier memory is of seeing my

4

father at prayer, on his knees by the side of his bed. To us children, it seemed as if he was there for hours and, getting impatient, we used to jump on his back as he tried to finish. This image of him at prayer has been an example and an inspiration to me all my life.

My father was born in the year 1895, in Java, of a French father and Dutch-Indonesian mother. He was given the name Célestin. His upbringing had been very French, and he would speak French to his father, Henri. His mother, Jeanne, was a beautiful woman, adored by her husband and family. At home she would dress in 'sarong and kebaya', as was the custom with Dutch women in those days. She died at the age of forty-eight, four months before I was born.

I was given her name, Jeanne, and perhaps because of this I feel very close to her at times. I treasure the few items in my possession that once belonged to Jeanne, and I love to feel them in my hands and touch them. Among them is a small leather purse containing a lock of dark brown hair. I often open the purse and touch the thick strands of hair and let my mind wander. My grandfather was a sentimental man and I picture Henri cutting this lock of hair, at a time perhaps when Jeanne was asleep, when he knew that she would not be with him much longer because of her illness. This lock of hair was something of her that he would always have and treasure.

Henri's beautiful house and all its contents were destroyed in the war, but this small leather purse he kept close to his heart till his dying days.

I adored Henri. He had come to Java at the age
of eighteen and spoke fluent Dutch with a charming
French accent. He was a hard-working man and
always walked with a straight back. Even at the age
of seventy-seven he still did his daily exercises and
could touch his toes without bending his knees!

All my school holidays were spent at my grandfather's place in Bandoengan, where he owned a
holiday resort, three thousand feet up on the slopes
of Oengaran mountain, in central Java. During holiday time, it was a relief for my mother to exchange the
hot climate of Tjepiering for the cool mountain air of
Bandoengan.

This lovely house in Bandoengan is engraved in
my memory forever. I remember every room, every
corner — the ornamental floor tiles and the loose
rugs, the gaslights on the wall, which the houseboy
lit each evening with ceremonial precision. I remember the pictures on the wall and the ornaments, the
cane chairs and table, and my grandfather's desk in
the corner of the room, littered with family photos.
Most important of these was an enormous photograph of grandmother Jeanne, standing on an easel,
adorned on each side by two small pots of purple
gloxinias.

I can still hear Aunty Bets' slippered footsteps
as she busied herself around the house. Aunty Bets
was very special. She had taken over the household
duties after the death of Henri's wife, and she was like

6

a grandmother to us. She was a spinster aunt and to her we were like the children she had never had. She loved us deeply and always covered up for us if we got into trouble with our grandfather.

Henri's house was not only large enough for our family but for our Batavia cousins as well. Our days were spent in the swimming pools, on the tennis court, or climbing the mountain. In the evening, we sat around the table, playing games while my grandfather sat behind his desk, catching up with correspondence and paper-work.

He had a lovely singing voice and taught us many French songs. As small children we sat on his lap while he sang French nursery songs to us. Every Sunday morning, the French national anthem was played on the gramophone, while a loudspeaker piped the Marseillaise right throughout the grounds. Yes, dear old Henri remained a Frenchman at heart, even after he took Dutch nationality. My memories of weekends and holidays spent in this lovely place are the most precious and I only hope that heaven will contain one little corner just like Henri's resort in Bandoengan.

My mother, Josephine, was Dutch. I remember her as the graceful vine around the house, carrying on her arm a small basket in which she kept an enormous bunch of keys. All kinds of things would accumulate in this 'sleutel mandje', or key-basket. If we were looking for a small pair of scissors, a pencil, a rubber, a penknife, a button, a rubber-band or

7

handkerchief, we would find them in mother's key-basket. In later years she kept her glasses in it.

Her dressing table held a fascination for me. I have an image of her in my mind, sitting at the dressing table with the silver mirror, brush and comb set, which had been my father's wedding present to her. Alongside, there was a floral china bowl which held some of her jewellery and a small matching tray, filled with trinkets.

I loved playing with my mother's necklaces, sliding my fingers between the beads. I liked the amber necklace best because my father had bought it for her in the harbour of Port Said, on the long boat trip from Holland to Java. The amber beads were like love beads to me, and I often placed the necklace around my own neck. Knowing how I loved it, my mother gave me this amber necklace a few years before she died.

She had come out to Java from Holland as a young bride of twenty-three. She had met my father, Celestin, in Amsterdam, where he was studying to be an engineer. Looking at the photographs of him as a young man, I can imagine her falling hopelessly in love with him, for he was handsome!

Josephine gave birth to her first three children within five years of marriage. The first born was a son, Edouard, or Ward for short. Then followed my sister, Aline, and myself, Jeanne, or Jan as I was usually called. Eight years later she gave birth to my sister, Josephine, or Fien, while her last born was my youngest sister, Céleste.

My mother was truly loved by her family and we all have our special memories of her. She was always there for us and nothing was impossible for her. Like the time when I was allowed to have my first evening dress. I was seventeen years old and wanted to have a dress just like Deanna Durbin's. I had looked through many magazines and suddenly there it was, in *The Sketch*.

'Moeder, can I have this dress?' I asked, pointing to the picture of Deanna Durbin in layer upon layer of white tulle. 'It is not too hard to make, is it?'

'Of course not!' my mother answered and without a pattern she created this masterpiece for me.

I stood in front of the mirror when it was finished, turning round and round to see the layers of tulle swish and swirl. I felt so good! Imah, our cook, and Soemie, our housemaid, entered the room to share in the great moment of this, my first long evening dress. They gasped with admiration, their fingers lovingly stroking the many layers of white tulle, and said that 'nonni Jantje' was very 'bagoes', or beautiful, in her new dress. My mother made all our clothes, she was so clever with her scissors.

I was proud of my mother. Everyone was made welcome in our home and all my friends loved her. Our house was tastefully furnished, with beautiful paintings and artistic wall-hangings adorning the walls. Her touch was everywhere. She was a real home-maker and a perfect hostess, with a wonderful sense of humour. Both adults and children felt good in her presence for she always saw the good in people, rather than the negative characteristics. She never spoke a harsh word to us as children, leaving all that to my father.

Although I never saw her doing any real house-work during my childhood years, her hands were always busy, her time well-spent. Apart from the hours spent behind her Singer sewing machine and at the piano, Josephine had many other interests. She was in charge of the library at the Tjepiering Club and she did all the buying for the Club's store. She looked forward to the monthly calls of the sales representatives from the big cities of Batavia and Surabaya, and the news they provided.

The Club was the centre of social life for the sugar-factory estate. Apart from the library and the store, there was a lounge, a bar, a pool table, a billiard room and, of course, a dance floor. It was a place where the employees and their wives could meet and gossip, and relax over cool drinks.

Next to the Club was the tennis court, where children and adults played on separate days. It was an important moment in my life when, as a teenager, my tennis was considered good enough to play with the grown-ups. The big day arrived and I was invited to play my first game of tennis with the ladies. My mother had made me a new tennis skirt for the event. I was very nervous, in fact, terrified, and I tried to remember all the things my father had taught me.

The real test came at the end when one had to play a singles match with Mrs Eekhout, who was considered the best ladies' player. To my great surprise, I beat her, and at the end of the match she put her arms around me and brought me an 'ais-gosok', a flavoured drink of crushed ice, as a reward.

My parents were very much in love. Nevertheless, they had their arguments and quarrels. The good thing was that we always witnessed the 'making-up' afterwards, when they put their arms around each other. Then we would sigh with relief, feeling secure in the knowledge that they would always love one another.

The extended family

OUR FAMILY was made complete by the five Indonesian people who worked in our household. We employed a cook, a maid, a houseboy, a chauffeur and a gardener. I call them 'family' for that is what they were. Their devotion, loyalty and love were such that, merely by thinking of them, the tears will come into my eyes.

How can I ever find words to describe Imah, our cook, that gentle yet strong little woman, blind in one eye and always with a ready smile? Her capable hands produced the most superb 'ryst-tafel', which literally means 'rice-table'. My mother was proud of Imah and the more important the guests were at our dinner table the greater were the variety of dishes that Imah served. She was equally good at cooking a Dutch style dinner. In those far-off colonial days, a good cook was one of the most important assets of a household and my mother was often envied for having such a culinary expert as our Imah.

We children loved to spend time with her in the kitchen, squatting next to her on the floor, watching her crush and grind the 'bumbu' of chillies, coriander, cumin and other spices in the solid, round stone mortar. She let us take turns at turning the handle of the mincer and fanning the open charcoal stove with a 'kipas', or Indonesian fan. In Imah's domain we licked many saucepans and scooped our fingers into many of her delicious dishes.

Her son, Tjak, was our 'djongos' or houseboy. Always immaculately dressed, he served at the table, among his other jobs. He was an intelligent young man and very conscientious at what he was doing.

My father's greatest hobby was music and he taught Tjak how to take care of the numerous classical gramophone records, where to shelve them and how to find them. Tjak was fascinated by the strains of beautiful music that filled the house and he, too, developed a love of classical music and was extremely proud to be in charge of the gramophone player, turning the handle and changing the needles with the greatest of care. He had his own favourites among the records and it took him no time at all to come up with

Schubert's *Unfinished Symphony* or Rimsky Korsakov's *Scheherazade*.

This was a time when we had no telephones laid on in our homes on the Tjepiering estate. Instead, communication from house to house was established by way of the old-fashioned slate, which consisted of two slates, set in wooden frames and held together with hinges. This way the double slate could be opened and closed like a folder. A slate pencil was attached to the frame. My mother would write a message to a friend on the left-hand slate and the reply was then written on the slate on the right.

Tjak enjoyed running errands with the slate. It gave him an opportunity to chat with domestics from other households. While waiting for the written reply, he would be offered a cool drink before walking home with the slate under his arm, his head filled with the latest servants' gossip.

Also in our service was Soemie, a quiet woman, who loved to chew her 'sirih', or betel nut, while she kept our bedrooms spick and span. Soemie's domain was the 'soemoer', where she did all our washing by hand; her only tools a washboard and a bar of yellow soap.

The 'soemoer' was a well in the back garden, surrounded by a round, white wall, which had fragrant jasmin climbing over it. We children had a fascination for the 'soemoer', for it was a cool place and always smelt good. It also functioned as the perfect hiding place, much to Soemie's annoyance.

We knew that she had finished her washing when the 'whites' were laid out flat on the back lawn to bleach in the tropical sun. Soemie loved us dearly, perhaps because she had no children of her own. She had been widowed at a young age and never married again. I have fond memories of her sitting by the side of my bed singing 'Nina Bobo', an Indonesian lullaby, again and again, in her sweet, soft voice.

Our gardener was named Sardie. He cut our lawns by hand with an 'arrit', a special Indonesian cutting knife, and made them look as neat as a Wimbledon tennis court! My father's other great hobby was tropical fish and he had taught Sardie to help him take care of the many aquariums. If a fish died, it was poor Sardie who got the blame.

We children felt a bit sorry for Sardie. He was not very bright and this often got him into trouble. When my father had a bad day at work, Sardie always 'copped' it, but he took it all in his stride and never let go of his smile.

Finally, there was Ahmad. He was our chauffeur, looked upon by the others as having the most prestigious job in the O'Herne household. And he was proud of it! Ahmad kept our Chevrolet in immaculate condition; our car was his great pride and joy.

Our domestics shared all our food and my mother supplied them with neat clothes of their choice. She made sure they all received a new outfit for 'Tahun baru', the Indonesian New Year.

How we loved these devoted people, who shared our daily lives, in sickness and in health, in times of

14

tears and times of joy. They were truly part of our family. As children, we knew that we could cry on one of their shoulders if we were in trouble or needed some special help. It was Ahmad who taught my brother, Ward, to drive. It was Imah who taught me to cook a 'ryst-tafel', simply by allowing me to watch her in her kitchen. It was also Imah who cured all my mother's headaches. With her strong hands and clever technique, she massaged the pain away.

RECEIVING OVERSEAS mail was a high point shared by everyone in our household, when letters from my mother's family arrived once a month by boat. Tjak would give the letters to my mother on a small silver tray, making a joyful ceremony out of an otherwise routine event. He always recognised the letters from Holland.

'Soerat tanah blanda', or 'letter from Holland', was the usual announcement, his head nodding with approval, a smile beaming on his face. Tjak then waited and watched my mother nervously tear open the envelope, leaving again, unnoticed, when he was assured by her expression that the news was indeed happy.

I remember the time when the first aeroplanes began to fly the route from Holland to Java, delivering the first airmail letters on thin notepaper. The sheer excitement of it all! But these early aviation days were not without danger and I can clearly recall the disaster of the Dutch plane, the *Stuiver*, which crashed

15

and burst into flames. We received some of the retrieved airmail letters; the envelopes and pages partly burned at the corners. My mother tried to piece them together, the tears streaming down her face.

The vendors

OUR FAMILY loved 'terong blanda', the tamerillo fruit, which only grew in the cooler climate of the mountain hillsides. We had a Javanese vendor who came all the way down from the mountain, some 100 kilometres, just to sell his 'terong blanda'.

It took him about four days to walk down from the hillside, carrying the fruit in baskets, hanging from a yoke across his shoulders, a piece of rubber tied under his bare feet. He probably could have sold the tamerillos closer to home, but he preferred to walk the longer distance because he knew for certain that my mother would buy all his fruit.

The man would arrive totally exhausted and sometimes his teeth would be chattering from fever. We children looked upon him as a hero for making the great trek from the mountain. First he would be taken into the kitchen on the back verandah, where Imah gave him a bowl of rice and 'sayur', or vegetable soup, followed by a cup of strong black coffee.

He stayed the night before setting out on his long walk back, my mother giving him a fresh supply of quinine tablets and some treats for his children. Contented, a big grin across his weather-beaten face,

16

he wished us 'selamat tinggal', or goodbye, and we would already be looking forward to his next visit.

The other regular visitor we looked forward to coming to our home, was the Chinese 'Klontong' or door-to-door salesman. He sold beautiful hand-embroidered linen — tablecloths, serviettes, handkerchiefs and pillow cases, just to mention a few. He was a clever salesman and a very good talker.

'No, I don't need any more Chinese embroidery', was always my mother's first reaction.

'Moeder, can we just have a look?' we children begged.

Then we crowded round the 'Klongtong' as he spread out his magnificent wares. This ceremony could take up to half-an-hour, and it took just as long to pack it all again. My mother always ended up buying something and most of this beautiful linen was sent to Holland in Christmas parcels for the family. Some of it has survived, even to this day.

On many occasions, Javanese children came to the house to sell us their captured animals. Ward, Aline and I were always moved to tears at the sight of these poor creatures, cramped into a small basket, unable to move.

'Moeder, can we buy ... please, please?' we cried.

And so over the years we acquired quite a menagerie in our large back garden. Apart from our Alsatian dogs, we had an anteater, snakes, tortoises, birds, a stork, a deer, guinea pigs, a monkey, and chickens! These animals enriched our childhood years and taught us how to respect and care for God's creatures. The story of our stork, Jacob, is just one example.

One day a Javanese boy came to our house, trying to sell us his captured stork. The little stork looked out of the small basket and we could see that his beak was bleeding, as he tried to poke it out. We felt so sorry for this young bird. My mother, too, was moved by the pitiful sight. Giving the boy a twenty-five cent piece, we quickly took the bird out.

'What shall we call him?' we asked each other, deciding on the name, Jacob.

We fed Jacob with fish and with eels, which we caught specially for him and he soon grew up into a fine stork. He was very tame and quite happy in our garden and we all loved him, and didn't want to lose him.

My father clipped his wings a little bit and in this way he could still fly, but not fly away. He had his favourite spot, standing on the high white wall that surrounded our back garden.

Jacob did not always behave as he should. My mother used to keep a piece of soap in the wash-basin on the back verandah, and the stork took a liking to it. Perhaps he thought it was a fish! He pecked the soap up with his long beak and swallowed it whole, but luckily it did not seem to harm him.

He was so at home with us that my father decided it was not necessary to clip his wings any more, as we were sure he would not fly away. A year went by and then one day, when Jacob was perched on his high wall, he suddenly noticed a flock of large birds, flying high over our house. They were storks, like Jacob, migrating birds who flew to Java during their breeding time. We watched Jacob as he looked at the birds, flying high above us. Then suddenly, up he went, in flight, spreading out his wings to join the other birds.

It must have been a difficult decision for him to make, but he followed his instinct and we stood there, gazing up in the sky as Jacob joined his family. We were sad to see him go. We would miss him and all his antics — the clapping sound of his large beak and seeing him waiting on the verandah for his breakfast. But in another way we were happy for him and we really thought that we would never see him again.

Another year went by and my father was out, inspecting the sugar cane fields, with two of his Javanese workmen. Suddenly, one of the men pointed at the sky.

'Look, toean O'Herne, a flock of storks!'

Trailing behind, they could see one bird that looked like Jacob. Now it was circling above their heads. My father knew it was Jacob because he could see the uneven wings that had once been clipped.

He returned home, very excited and called us together.

'Guess what!' he said. 'Jacob has come back. I have seen him.'

'We know, we know', we cried out. 'Come, look in the back garden.'

There, on the top of the wall, in his favourite spot, stood Jacob. He looked at us as if he had never been away. It was as if he was saying, 'Come on, where's my dinner!'

Jacob never flew away after that time and he was our favourite pet for many more years.

With bells attached to his pikulan

FOR US, the most sought after vendor was the local sate man. With his portable kitchen, we could smell him miles away. He appeared in the streets after dark, bells attached to his 'pikulan', or shoulder kitchen, and little lanterns suspended from the yoke.

As soon as we heard his familiar shout, we ran to the front gate to call him in, then begged our parents to allow us to have this most delicious treat. We were only allowed to eat from this one particular sate man, and never again in my life have I tasted 'sate ayam' and 'sate babi' so good or tasted such luscious peanut sauce!

With plates in hand, we squatted around our friendly sate man and watched him grill the skewered pieces of meat over the charcoal fire. Even the smoke smelled good.

The first 'edition' of children

FOR EIGHT years I enjoyed being the youngest of my mother's first 'edition' of children. My big brother, Ward, was my hero, and we played well together. He rescued me from many difficult situations, like the time I fell into the river, or the time he killed a python that had crossed our path. He always found his way out of the jungle when we were lost on one of our hiking trips in the mountains and always knew what to do in emergencies. He was a perfect leader.

He made his own toy soldiers by melting down the lead and pouring it into various moulds. Afterwards, he painted the soldiers' uniforms, different colours for the different countries. I loved to watch my brother as he set out his soldiers on the verandah in front of his bedroom. He planned and created the most amazing battlefields. Rocks and sand and vegetation; it was all there on the verandah.

The French soldiers always won the battles. I was allowed to play with him if I followed all his instructions and orders but, of course, my battalions were always on the losing side.

Ward got his first pair of long trousers when he was in his last year at high school. We celebrated this as a big step in his life and we were all very proud of him, for he suddenly looked grown-up. Shortly after, when he had graduated from high school, he went to Holland to study at the K.M.A., the Royal Military College at Breda.

I might add here that Ward finally became a General in the Dutch Army.

I missed him terribly after he left. The house was never the same again. Ward had been such a big part of my happy childhood. The only good thing that came from him leaving home was that from now on my sister, Aline, and I would both have our own bedrooms. She, being the eldest, got the room with the little verandah, much to my envy.

Aline was very clever with her hands and very artistic. If one of us in the family had a birthday, the tradition was that we would decorate his or her chair at the dinner table. She was always the best at this, using flowers, greenery, crepe paper and coloured ribbons — a different design each time.

She was the quiet one in the family, the gentle one. I looked up to her for she was wise in a way and always knew what was best, which at times infuriated me. She helped me with my homework and often took on the role of mother to me. If I dared not ask my mother a question, I could always ask her.

It was Aline, for example, who came to my rescue, seeing my bewildered face when I woke up one morning and found I had started my first period. I had wondered about those small, mysterious looking towels that were kept on the top shelf where I couldn't quite see them. Aline reached up to the top shelf of the wardrobe and handed me a home-made sanitary pad. In her efficient, casual sort of way, she explained that from now on I would have this sort of thing every month. Then she showed me how to put the towel on.

'You're a big girl now', she said lovingly, and patted me on the head. And that was about all the sex instruction I received. I could not understand why the spots of blood on my pants had suddenly transformed me into a 'big' girl.

'Jan has started her periods', I heard Aline say to my mother later that day. 'It's all right. I've told her all about it.'

My mother was probably quite relieved about that. What she did not know, however, was that Aline had not explained the purpose behind the monthly periods, with their relationship to sexual intercourse, conception and birth.

With our mother making all our dresses, we always looked smart and had no reason to complain. But all the same I was envious of girlfriends who had 'bought' dresses.

I was about fifteen years old when the news came that Aunty Corrie had opened a dress shop in Semarang, where she lived with her husband Uncle Henri. My mother couldn't wait to see Corrie's new shop and Ahmad, our chauffeur, took us there the following Saturday morning. I couldn't believe my eyes when I saw the rows and rows of pretty dresses, hanging on their rails.

'All imported from America!' said Aunty Corrie.

'American dresses!' I gasped. 'These must be just like the film stars wear.'

My fingers touched the adorable dresses.

'You girls can both choose one', said Aunty Corrie, seeing my wonderment.

'Really, can we really have one of these?' we said, looking at each other and then at my mother and Aunt Corrie.

It was a moment of sheer, absolute delight as Aline and I looked through all the dresses that were about our size. With the excitement of it all my heart was beating faster with anticipation, and then ... there it was! I pulled out the lovely pale green cotton dress with a pattern of tiny flowers on it. The dress had short puffed sleeves and on each side of the bodice there was a diamond shaped insert of lace. Till my dying days I will love and remember this, my first real 'bought' dress. For the first time in my life I possessed a dress with a little label at the back.

Maalfeest

LIVING ON a sugar factory estate brought great excitement at times, especially at the time of the 'Maalfeest', or harvest festival, which celebrated the first sugar cane entering the factory for production. Festivities, involving both the Dutch and the Indonesian communities, went for days on end.

An enormous 'Selamatan' dinner, with entertainment, was given for all the Javanese workmen. There was a 'Barongan', life-size marionettes with men inside, and a dragon, which frightened me as a child. We loved the 'Pasar malam', or night market and show, but the highlight was the famous 'Maalfeest' Ball, which people came from all over to attend.

The ball was held in a spacious area inside the sugar factory and my father, being a splendid organiser and creative artist, was responsible for turning the floor space into a ballroom. Assisted by dozens of skilful Javanese workmen, he brought about amazing transformations, designing the most imaginative surroundings, creating the most exotic atmosphere.

One year it was a 'Birds' Paradise', with brightly coloured birds and huge, bird-shaped paper lanterns, that lit up the ballroom. Another year, it was an Egyptian desert, decorated with sphinxes and pyramids. At yet another, a Paris nightclub, 'Le Chat Noir', with large black cats everywhere.

I was sixteen by the time I was considered old enough to attend the Maalfeest ball. My mother made us new dresses for the occasion and Aline, being older than me, had a full-length evening dress. Mine was three-quarter length, for I was not yet old enough to wear a long dress. It was one of the most exciting and important events of my teenage years.

Like a real wallflower, I sat with the other young girls along the wall, never expecting that I would get to dance, except with my father. I was perfectly content just to watch all the grown ups having a good time.

Then I saw a handsome young man enter the

ballroom with his parents. My mouth fell open in amazement. I had never seen such a good-looking young man before, except, of course, in movies. Word soon spread that he was twenty-six, the son of a newly arrived family at Tjepiering; that his name was Fred and that he lived and worked in Semarang.

The music started for the first dance and I watched the dance floor fill with couples as the band played 'Goody Goody'. Then Fred began to walk over to us girls, seated along the wall.

'Who will he ask to dance?' was the thought in each girl's mind.

He stood in front of me and bowed.

'Can I have this dance?' he said.

I blushed as I stammered a reply, hardly able to believe it.

'I am not a very good dancer', I said.

The next moment I was floating over the dance floor in his arms. We danced all night and oh, how wonderful it was to be sixteen years old at this, my first ball!

The hillside farm at Ampel Gading

WARD, ALINE and I loved swimming and tennis but the sport we enjoyed even more was climbing the mountain and hillsides near Bandoengan. The Oengaran mountain had two smaller side peaks, the Lapak and the Gendol. We climbed both to the

26

top, even though no one had ever been recorded as reaching the top of Gendol before. To prove that we had reached the summit, we used mirrors to signal to our family and friends below. We would leave first thing in the morning and be back before dark, our legs covered in cuts and scratches.

Our other favourite walks were to the Hindu temples at Gedong Songo, high up in the hills, and to a hillside farm at Ampel Gading, which belonged to a Japanese farmer and his wife. On arrival at the farmhouse, we were warmly greeted and cordially invited into the house. The Japanese couple gave us fresh milk from their cows and showed us around their farm. They were very friendly and always appreciated our visits. We were amazed when, at the onset of war in Java, this Japanese couple turned out to be spies. Their farm at the top of the hillside had a perfect view over vast strategic areas.

Many Japanese businessmen appeared on the scene in the years leading up to the Japanese invasion of Java. They were planted there on purpose to get ready for the forthcoming invasion. Our friendly Japanese photographer turned out to be a spy too. He was the most popular photographer in Semarang and he had taken several of our family photos. While these people had been bowing and smiling at us, they had been preparing for our destruction!

Bodjong

MY SCHOOL days took place at the Franciscan primary school, situated in Bodjong, the main street in Semarang. It took one hour, each morning, to reach there on the school bus.

School began at seven in the morning and finished at one o'clock. This meant that we returned home during the hottest part of the day. Overcome by the midday heat, our Indonesian driver had a tendency to nod off to sleep at the wheel, so we children took it in turns to sit beside him, watching him closely and poking him in the ribs with an elbow if he closed his eyes and nodded his head.

The Franciscan sisters were strict, but we loved and respected them. During the time of the Great Depression, my father's salary had been reduced by half and the good nuns allowed us to stay at school, without paying fees.

I visited my old primary school again for the first time in 1993. Although it had expanded enormously, the main part of the old building had changed very little. It was a magical feeling to be walking again on the same marble floor of the entrance hall. Pre-war photographs of the former Dutch sisters were hanging on the wall and nostalgic tears came into my eyes as I recognised some of them.

Directly below the photographs I recognised an old, marble-topped table that used to stand in the office of the headmistress, Sister Xavier. Looking at this table, I remembered the day fifty-eight years ago when I stood in utter disgrace in front of it.

I was in Grade Seven and the third of the O'Herne children to be in dear Sister Xavier's class. Arriving at school early one morning, I went into my classroom and noticed that the questions for our history test were written on the back of the easel blackboard. I couldn't believe my luck! Although the blackboard had been cunningly turned upside down, with a twist of the head I could still read the questions. I had started to jot them down when I heard the unmistakable tinkling of rosary beads. It was too late; in walked Sister Xavier, catching me in the act. I could feel myself blushing, dreadfully ashamed.

'How dare you do such a deceitful thing!' she reprimanded. 'You, Jan, of all pupils, and you an O'Herne at that.'

I felt I had disgraced the whole family and I really did not understand why I had committed this awful, dishonest deed. History was one of my best subjects and I would have known the answers anyway. But there it was. I had committed the sin and Sister Xavier made sure I would not forget it in a hurry. She told me to come to her office after school. So, there I stood, at the marble table, head down in shame, listening to all the virtues that twelve-year-old girls should have. Dishonesty was not one of them.

Sister Xavier was such a clever teacher. She would never have given us meaningless lines to write but always punished us with something that was beneficial at the same time. I could see the New Testament lying on the marble-topped table.

'Pick up that book', she said, 'and find St Paul's letter to the Ephesians, Chapter 5'.

I took the New Testament in trembling hands and fumbled through the pages.

'Look more at the back', Sister said. 'The letters of St Paul start after the Acts.'

'That's all right if you know where the Acts are', I thought, frantically turning more pages. With a bit more help from Sister Xavier, I found the Ephesians, Chapter 5.

'Now, read to me. Verse 7 to verse 14', she said in her calm voice. 'And read it out, loud and clear.'

'You were darkness once', I began, 'but now you are light in the Lord; be like children of light, for the effects of the light are seen in complete goodness and right living and truth.

'Try to discover what the Lord wants of you, having nothing to do with the futile works of darkness but exposing them by contrast. The things which are done in secret are things that people are ashamed even to speak of; but anything exposed by the light will be illuminated and anything illuminated turns into light.'

I looked up at Sister Xavier wondering what was next.

'Now learn that off by heart', she said, signalling me to leave.

Although I did not have to recite these verses

from the Ephesians the next day, the result was the same and they were imprinted in my mind. Trust a Franciscan to give me a punishment such as this, laying the seed for my great love of scripture.

From the tender care of the Franciscan sisters I moved on to the H.B.S., the High School of Semarang, also situated on Bodjong. It was a co-educational school, a colonial-style building, with large pillars and wide steps, leading up to the front entrance. Tall native trees provided plenty of shade in the yard and on either side of the main building were wings, housing more classrooms. The shady verandahs and passage ways gave plenty of opportunities for leisurely strolls with school friends. We had splendid teachers and I made wonderful friends; friendships which have lasted to this day. They were happy days, without a care in the world, a sheltered environment in which I grew up as part of an innocent generation when girls were still virgins on their wedding day.

AFTER FINISHING high school I found myself adjacent to my old primary school again, attending the Frans-ciscan Teachers' College. Thus all my preparatory teaching was done at my former school.

The Fransciscan nuns had a great influence on me. We had many lay teachers but subjects like music, history, language and psychology were taught by the nuns. Religious education, church history and theology were given by the Jesuit priests from the seminary.

The nuns invoked my curiosity. Mysteriously hidden behind veil and habit, they radiated an aura of serenity, purity and peace. I always arrived at college very early and, sneaking into the chapel, I used to watch them at prayer. Somehow, seeing them lost in meditation helped me to pray too.

How I loved the sound of bells, ringing through the convent and college corridors, spilling over joyfully into the grounds where a large statue of the Sacred Heart, arms outstretched, looked over us with love. When the Angelus bell rang at twelve midday, we stopped whatever we were doing and recited the Angelus prayer together.

The Angelus had a most soothing effect on me. It was a moment of stillness in the middle of busy activities. In the midst of action and the hustle and bustle of the day, there was this breathing space of contemplation and calmness.

Singing was my favourite relaxation. Our music teacher, Sister Laetitia, taught me the magnificent art of singing the Gregorian chant. Just by watching her conduct, I knew how to sing.

With my head filled with religion, bells, nuns, church music, prayer and homilies on the virtues of purity, it was no wonder that I realised I had a vocation for the religious life. Nurtured by the nuns, my vocation gave me great joy of heart. When I told Sister Laetitia that I wanted to be a nun, she was delighted.

'You'll make a good nun', she assured me, giving me the next day, a holy picture of the 'Pieta'. On the back she had written a special prayer for me. I still have this holy picture today.

To encourage my vocation I was now allowed to go into the Sisters' extensive library and borrow their books. Only the nuns knew of my intentions. I had not yet told anyone else.

War in Europe and the fall of Singapore

IT WAS during my years at Teachers' College that war began to rage through Europe. On 10 May 1940, German troops invaded Holland. Four days later, the Dutch surrendered. We were all very concerned about our families in Holland, thinking we were so lucky to be living in the Dutch East Indies, and that war would never come to us here.

Everyone was now helping towards the war effort in Europe. At our school, we held functions and concerts to raise funds for the 'spitfire' planes of the British R.A.F. Each morning, as soon as I arrived at college, I listened to the radio for the latest news on the war.

Pearl Harbour was bombed by the Japanese on 7 December 1941. The next morning I heard the news on the college radio.

'Now, perhaps the Americans will start fighting', Sister Victoire, our history teacher, commented.

I will always remember that morning. It was 8 December, the feast of the Immaculate Conception of the Blessed Virgin Mary. Suddenly, the war had come closer. Soon after, the Philippines fell to the Japanese but we were still hoping we were safe in Java. My father was forty-seven years old at the time and had already been called up for military service earlier that year, and so my mother was left alone to make all the decisions at this difficult time.

ON 15 February 1942 Singapore surrendered. With the fall of Singapore, we in Java knew that it was only a matter of time before the Japanese attacked our shores. The whole country was now preparing for war. With so much uncertainty, nobody knew what to do for the best.

My grandfather suggested that it would be best for us to come and stay with him in the mountains of Bandoengan. Thus, my mother, myself and my sisters, Fien and Céleste, prepared to leave our home. Living with our grandfather, we would at least be far away from the coast.

Our domestics were very upset. My mother gave them all a big advance in salary but she could not tell them when we would come back.

'In any case', she said, 'nonni Aline will come up and see you and keep in touch'.

My sister, Aline, was living in Semarang, working there for the Netherlands East Indies Railways (N.I.S.). My mother was very nervous. She missed my father in the decision making. Seeing her crying, I realized that I had to be her pillar of strength from now on.

We packed as much as we could fit into the car, not knowing if we could ever come back to our lovely home. Ahmad, our chauffeur, was coming with us and would take us on the two-hour drive to Bandoengan. Treasured possessions, things of sentimental value, my mother's jewellery, a few photo albums and clothes were all nervously packed into the car, which was to make two trips.

I looked around my room to see what I would take. Suddenly, everything took on a new meaning. It became so precious because I had to part with it and leave it behind. I took my crucifix from the wall; it would not take up much room in my case. I packed my bible, prayer book and rosary beads, and the book of Saints that had recently been given to me after I had made my first retreat.

I opened my wardrobe to decide what clothes to take. I looked at my first long evening dress. Because of the many layers of tulle, it would take up too much room. I held the dress in front of me and looked in the mirror. Then I put it back on its hanger with tears in my eyes. Eventually, I packed a few old favourites and carefully folded them in my suitcase. Little did I know that these dresses had to last me for the next three and a half years.

The time had come to say goodbye to our beloved household family, Imah, Soemie, Tjak and Sardie. They had been part of our family all our lives. Tjak assured my mother that he would keep an eye on our house and take care of the dog until Aline could collect him. Something inside me told me that I was never to see our house and these beloved friends again.

Everyone was in tears as we started to say our farewells. We embraced and clung to each other desperately. Our cook, Imah, seemed to totally disappear in my arms, she was so little. Imah had always been my favourite. I could find no words to thank her for all the beautiful meals she had cooked for us; the special treats she would always have ready for us after school; the many hours we had spent in her kitchen, tasting her delicacies and dipping our fingers in the home made peanut butter and 'ontbytkoek' cake batter. We couldn't believe that we had to leave our home and these beautiful people behind. Then Ahmad held open the door and one by one we squeezed into the car and drove off. It was the end of an era.

In Bandoengan

OUR GRANDFATHER was glad to have us with him in Bandoengan. In these uncertain times it was best for all of us to stay together. We had only been with him a short time when orders were issued by our government. When warning of a Japanese landing came, all resources that would be useful to the Japanese army were to be destroyed. In due course, when this happened, bridges were blown up and trains, boats, motor vehicles, trucks, horses and machinery — all were destroyed.

It was my father's habit before breakfast each morning at Tjepiering to ride his beautiful Australian horse, Jack. He was an excellent rider and this was his greatest joy, his greatest relaxation. Knowing his love for the horse, we had transported Jack to Bandoengan and kept him at the stables of a friend who lived quite close to grandfather. Following orders, we realised that the horse and also our car would have to be destroyed.

When Jack was shot I could not stand to watch it happen. I remember hearing the rifle shot and it seemed as if it had been aimed at my father.

My mother had to tell Ahmad the bad news about our beautiful car. My father had bought a brand new Renault only a year before. Ahmad had been so proud of it, looking after it with the greatest of care. He had kept 'his' car immaculate, inside and out.

He looked at my mother in disbelief. He had no

intention of destroying 'his' car and he flatly refused to do so. In the end my mother had to find someone else to do it. I felt so sorry for Ahmad. His whole life, his whole world, went up with that car. Bit by bit we had to part with more possessions, and this was only the beginning.

The Nippon flag was hoisted everywhere

I WAS nineteen years old when on 1 March 1942 the Japanese troops invaded Java. The Dutch put up a good fight but had to surrender to the Japanese on 8 March. The Nippon flag was hoisted everywhere. It was the end of a colonial period that had lasted for more than three centuries.

The months that followed were frightening and put a strain on everyone. It was all too much for our dear Aunty Bets. She, who had spent her whole life caring for others, died in my arms after a short illness.

Up to now, because we were living in the mountains, we had not seen any Japanese close up — only at a distance, as Japanese army trucks passed by. Then, the alarming order came that all Europeans had to assemble at a certain place for registration and we saw our first Japanese soldier close up. We arrived at the place of registration, bowed politely and filled in the form: nationality, country of birth, age, gender, profession etc. We handed in our pieces of paper and returned home with fear in our hearts.

It was not long afterwards that we heard military trucks coming up the hill towards grandfather's house. Soon one truck was in the driveway leading up to the house. Two Japanese soldiers jumped off. Heavy booted, bayonets fixed in position, they walked towards us. It was a terrifying moment.

They came onto the front verandah, shouting loudly. We were told to pack and get ready to leave for prison camp. Long fearing this moment, we had already packed away our most important papers and possessions. With the soldiers looking on, we nervously packed our cases. We were allowed one suitcase and one mattress each. The time allowed was short and it was difficult to decide what to take and what to leave behind. But if I had to pack that suitcase again now, I would know just what to put in it. I would fill it with medicine, quinine tablets, calcium tablets, halibut liver oil, soap, powdered milk and candles. But how were we to know at such a moment?

Henri was to remain at his home. He had entered on his registration form that he was French, and German and French people were not interned. It was heartbreaking to say goodbye to him. I had spent all my school holidays in his loving care. In Bandoengan, he had given me the happiest moments of my childhood. He spoke to me in French as he held me in his arms. I loved him so much at that moment. Look after your 'maman', he said. Then he made the sign of the cross on each of our foreheads.

"Toujours quand-meme — Always, in spite of everything", he said, trying to be brave.

The next moment we were loaded onto the waiting truck. My grandfather waved his white handkerchief as the truck drove away.

We picked up more women and children until the truck could hold no more. What a pitiful sight we were, packed together like sheep! My mother, Fien, Céleste and I sat close together as the truck drove down the hill towards Ambarawa. Once again we had to leave behind people we loved and a house that held happy memories. I was to spend the next three and a half years in captivity, together with my mother and sisters and many thousands of Dutch women and children, my childhood dreams shattered.

Part 2

The Ambarawa Camp

THE TRUCK moved slowly towards our new destination, Ambarawa prison camp. Javanese men, women and children waved to us as we passed them on the road. I wondered what was going through their minds, seeing us being carted away in this manner. Ambarawa was not far from Bandoengan and we knew the place well. We used to go to Church and often did our shopping there as well.

The truck slowed down as we approached the camp and as the gates opened we knew immediately that we were entering a prison. The Japanese military were shouting orders at us. We got off the truck as best we could, but we had no idea what they were saying, which got us into trouble straight away. Children started to cry and, as the women tried to get their suitcases and bags down, the mattresses fell in the mud. Our hearts sank as we looked around.

The camp was comprised of old, abandoned army barracks, which had not been used for some time — row upon row of them. We lined up at a table with two Japanese sitting behind it. A basket stood ready for all money, jewellery and other valuables to be surrendered.

Most women were reluctant to do this, and so we were searched. I was wearing my mother's jewellery under my clothing, in a belt, sewn especially for this purpose, around my bare waist. As my turn approached, I became very nervous but they did not do a thorough body search and so the jewellery was not found.

Dragging our luggage and mattresses, we made our way over to the barracks. There were tears in my mother's eyes as she saw the appalling conditions.

'We can't live here, the whole place is filthy!' one of the women cried out.

So, before doing anything, we began to clean up. It was not an easy task and the realisation sunk in that this terrible place was to be our new home.

We were in Kamp 6, a damp barracks, infested with bugs, lice and cockroaches, with rotten wood-work and a leaking roof. The place was plagued by rats and at night we could feel them, literally running over our toes and even nibbling at them. There was little water and not enough taps, which meant queuing up for every drop. The worst of it, however, was the appalling sanitation and the stench and dysentery that resulted.

Invariably, we would be awakened during the night by the sound of bladders being emptied in chamber pots, buckets or pans. We got to recognise the different sounds of 'streams' or 'trickles'. But there was one that was most distinctive. We called its originator 'the Hose'.

The barracks had been designed to hold a couple of hundred soldiers. Now there were thousands of women and children using the same ghastly lavatories, if you could call them that. Overflowing sewerage continually spilled out into the compound.

Although there were some bunks in the barracks, they were infested with bugs, unusable. We were allotted a small space, barely big enough to lay out our mattresses. During the daytime, we stacked them, one on top of the other, to provide a place to sit. There was no electricity laid on and as soon as it began to get dark we lit candles.

Thanks to my mother's ingenuity, we created a measure of privacy by hanging sheets between families, partitioning us off. But we never had any real privacy and could always overhear the crying of babies and children, and the conversations, quarrels and arguments. We were lucky enough, however, to have some very nice women and children as 'neighbours'. Their friendship was invaluable.

How can I ever find the right words to describe this, our first night in the prison camp? It marked the end of everything that had been good, beautiful and secure, and the beginning of fear and uncertainty. How long would we be kept here? Would we ever see our loved ones again? Where was my father, was he still alive? We were all so tired out and yet we could not sleep, so we just lay there, overcome by the shock and the sudden change in our lives.

Lying there, in the flickering candlelight, looking at the decaying rafters of the roof, I could not help thinking of the lovely family home we had left behind. We said our prayers together, something the four of us continued to do each night from then on. I looked in my mother's prayer book for something suitable,

44

but there was no such thing as a prayer for those in
captivity.

'We still have each other', my mother whispered
in the darkness, trying to cheer us up. 'Surely the
war will soon be over.'

The art of bowing deeply

THE NEXT day we were summoned for our first roll
call. From then on, this was a daily routine. We were
taught the art of bowing deeply from the waist down.
Roll call was Nippon's opportunity to let us know how
inferior we were and who was in command. Orders
were given. Women and children were counted,
beaten, humiliated, and kept standing for hours in
the sun.

Life in the camp was very much according to the
moods and whims of the camp commandant and
guards. On that first morning we were ordered never
to leave camp. Women were to work hard and be
obedient. If not, they would be punished, beaten, or
even killed. And we would always have to bow to
Nippon.

For the smooth running of the camp, we immediately got ourselves organised and appointed a
camp head. Work shifts were set up, the young
women doing the hard, manual labour. The older
women were given easier tasks, like working in the
communal kitchen. We younger ones unloaded

45

trucks, carried heavy loads and sacks, chopped wood and dug holes. We cleaned the overflowing toilets, the wash-house and latrines, and kept our barracks and compound as clean as possible and in good repair.

We had a female doctor and nurses and we made our own makeshift hospital, without medical supplies. Quinine tablets were the most precious weapon against malaria and those who entered the camp with a good supply were the lucky ones.

FROM NOW on, food was the great obsession, and as our rations got worse over the years so did our hunger pains. We lived on a starvation diet. Breakfast, a watery porridge made out of starchy flour. Dinner, a small serving of rice with a watery vegetable soup. At night, a hard slice of bread. We used to soak it in water to make it more palatable. Babies were dying rapidly because there was no milk. Mothers' breast milk dried up and they watched helplessly as their little ones died.

We never received any meat or fat, butter, eggs or milk, or any high protein or vitamin rich food. My little sister, Céleste, used to eat her food with a teaspoon to make it last longer. Sometimes bananas came into the camp but by the time they were divided between the hospital, the babies and the small children, you were lucky if you even got to smell one.

I remember when it was Céleste's turn. Her little face lit up with delight as she was given half of one banana. This she shared with Fien. The banana

46

skins were never thrown away, but also eaten and sometimes fried in candle wax. You had to eat it quickly before the wax set in your mouth.

The children scavenged in the Japanese rubbish bins for banana peel, chicken bones and other food scraps. We used to boil up the bones for soup. Scavenging became so popular that the children had to take it in turns to fight over the bones.

One day, when it happened to be our family's turn for extra food, some offal was delivered to the kitchen: buckets filled with intestines, ears, eyes and anything slippery and horrible that you can think of. I was allowed to choose something out of the bucket and putting in my hand, I pulled out the first thing I got hold of.

'Look Mum!' I said excitedly, 'Something to make soup!'

My mother burst out laughing when she saw what I had picked out.

'Those are bull's testicles!' she said, 'They'll be full of goodness.'

And indeed, we made a beautiful soup with rich yellow rings of fat floating on the top. The testicles were boiled several times more for soup before we eventually ate them. They tasted quite good. We learned to eat anything that was not likely to kill us. Snails, and weeds with juicy stems.

THE CAMP commandant had a beautiful white cat that looked better fed than any of us and when the commandant took the daily roll call, the cat always followed him into the compound. As I watched this beautiful pussy cat curling itself around the commandant's legs, a tempting thought entered my mind. The cat would make a lovely dinner for those who were sick in our camp hospital. It could even save someone's life. I talked it over with some of my friends and we decided to try and catch it at the first opportunity.

One morning, when the usual roll call ritual of bowing, counting, and bowing again was over, I noticed that pussy had wandered away from her master, who was busy shouting at one of the women for not bowing deeply enough.

'Puss, puss, pussy', I called softly.

To my delight the cat responded, coming over to where I was standing, somewhere in the back rows. I grabbed her quickly, my heart pounding in my breast. What had I done! It would surely mean the death penalty if I was found out.

The commandant left the compound, not even missing his beloved cat. We dispersed, and within no time, pussy was boiling away in the pot. The dear cat supplied a splendid dinner for some of the sick in the hospital. We boiled and re-boiled her bones until no more soup would come from them.

In the meantime, a big search went on for poor pussy. Our commander was suspicious but he never really found out what had happened. The punishment came when our meagre ration of bread was brought into the camp and we were ordered to dig a

48

big hole and bury it. That night, we dug most of it out, shook off the sand and ate it.

We lived under continual strain and fear and as a result people were not always nice to each other in the camp. If it was a matter of survival, women would steal from each other to keep their children alive. Even the children learned to cheat and steal and be dishonest, just to get that bit of extra food.

The most sought after work duty was to help in the kitchen. Here was a chance to eat some raw vegetables or hide food in the pockets of clothes. A watch group was always on duty to make sure that the women rostered did an honest day's work.

One day, when my mother was too sick to take her turn in the kitchen, I took her place, sitting next to Riek, who was always good company. We were chopping away at the vegetables while Riek kept me up to date with the latest rumours and camp gossip.

'Kangkong again', she said.

'Kangkong', a small green leaf vegetable, was our daily food, for it was the cheapest vegetable and grew like a weed. It did not taste too good but at least it contained plenty of vitamins and iron in its green stems and leaves.

Chop, chop, chop went our knives. Suddenly, a lizard fell from the roof onto Riek's chopping board. It did not stand a chance. In no time its head was severed among the 'kangkong' leaves. Next, its body was chopped into thin slices under Riek's ruthless knife. Now there was only the wriggly tail left.

'Got you!', laughed Riek, as she sliced the tail in neat little pieces. Then she tipped her board towards the big pot.

'At least we'll have some meat in our soup today', she said.

Easter 1943

IT WAS our first Easter in the camp.

'Do you think the children will get eggs at Easter?', asked eight-year-old Céleste.

I don't know what made me say it, but I answered, 'Yes, Céleste. Somehow you will have your Easter Egg.'

I knew only too well that it was most unlikely that eggs were going to be delivered to the camp. Apart from that, it was not even Fien and Céleste's turn to get them. But it happened that it was my turn to clean out the guards' latrines and that close by there was a fowl pen, belonging to the Japanese and strictly out of bounds for prisoners.

The chickens in the pen were the skinniest chooks imaginable. Furthermore, they had never been known to lay eggs. I cleaned out the latrines and then, out of sheer curiosity, I went over to the fowl pen. Nobody had ever dared to steal one of the Japs' chickens and I was quite nervous just looking at them. Then I saw it ... a tiny white egg! I quickly looked around to see if anyone had seen me.

Carefully I stretched my hand through an opening in the wire netting. I could just reach the egg. Hiding it under my blouse, I walked casually back to our barracks. I felt as if everybody could see I was concealing a forbidden treasure. Nobody had seen me take it and I told no one.

I boiled the egg and decorated it as best I could. Fien and Céleste had their egg that Easter. From then on, I truly believed in the saying, 'God will provide'.

The children were our greatest concern. It was important that they be kept as happy as possible, which was not always easy with most of the mothers irritable, sick or stressed out. We set up a school and I found myself teaching without books, paper and pencils, learning enough about teaching to last me the rest of my life.

As a reward the mothers sometimes gave me a slice of bread, or anything that had trading value. At school time I tried to teach the children to be honest and never to steal someone else's food. One little boy put up his hand.

'Is it all right Miss, to steal from the Japanese?' he asked.

I am afraid I did not have an answer for that one.

'We will leave that for the Lord to decide', I replied.

The children were without fathers and those whose mothers had died were left to the mercy and kindness of other prisoners. For some young children, and for those who were born in the camps, this

51

was the only world they had ever known. One little girl only knew her father as a photograph and each time she saw a picture, or someone's photo, she cried out, 'Daddy, daddy!'.

The children soon learned to fend for themselves and to guard their food at all times. One morning we heard army vehicles arriving at the camp. We could tell by the bowing and scraping of the guards that high ranking military had arrived.

The news spread that a load of biscuits had arrived for the children and they were to come up to the front by the office, and receive their share. Within no time they were there, jumping up and down in anticipation. Some didn't even know what biscuits were. Tables were carried out and plates with biscuits were placed around, temptingly. The children crammed around the table, eagerly looking at the biscuits. A photographer appeared and they were told to smile. As soon as the pictures were taken, the biscuits were removed. It had all been one big propaganda stunt. The children were lucky if they managed to get even one!

One of the saddest cruelties inflicted by the Japanese was that as soon as a boy reached twelve he had to leave his mother and the women's camp, and move into the men's. Naturally, many of the women tried to lie about the age of their boys, but I still had several friends who had to give up their sons and brothers that way. Each time there were heart-breaking scenes. The mothers were hysterical, and the boys cried their hearts out as the Japanese took them away in a truck. Some of the guards were kind to the children one moment and just as cruel the next.

Tenko

THE JAPANESE knew that the women still had jewellery and money and therefore they made countless inspections of our living quarters, always without warning. There would be a sudden 'tenko', or roll call, and while we stood for hours in the sun the guards searched our barracks and belongings. The women hid their valuables in different places all the time and punishments were severe if anything forbidden was found. Not only the offending women but the whole camp would be punished. It could mean the withdrawal of food, standing an extra hour in the sun, burying our food, or witnessing the woman in question being beaten. So we had to be very careful about our hiding places.

One of our friends was a cripple, with one leg shorter than the other, and so needed special shoes. One shoe had a much higher heel than the other, making it the perfect hiding place for jewellery. We had it down to a fine art, with jewellery hidden in the roof, under the ground, in the hems of dresses; even in one's hair bun, or concealed somewhere on the body.

One day we had to hand in all our books for

inspection. Some of these were confiscated but others were returned with a Japanese sticker pasted on the front cover. My *Book of Saints* and my old prayer books still have these little Japanese labels on the front, now faded and unreadable.

Each night, before we went to sleep, I read a story out of the *The Lives of God's Beloved Saints for every day of the year*. Fien and Céleste loved this special story time, and I can assure you that the lives of the saints were far from boring.

On 23 December, I was reading the story of St Servulus, a beggar; a poor, disabled man who had no possessions at all. We were all touched by the story and could readily identify with it. At the end of the reading my mother pointed at her old patched-up bed jacket and said, with a sense of humour that was typical of her, 'Look! I am almost as poor as Saint Servulus!'.

We roared with laughter and from that day on, my mother's old bed jacket was referred to as her 'Servulus jasje', or 'Servulus jacket'. She could never part with it and I believe my sister, Fien, still has it to this day.

A very close bond developed between mother, Fien, Céleste and myself. We shared so many joys and sorrows and sufferings during those war years. We had each other, and our family love sustained us. This was the very thing denied to the husbands and fathers in their prisoner of war camps. They did not have the children with them. The women always had

54

their children to live for and to fight for but the men were lonely, missing the companionship of the children. More men died in the camps than women. It is a fact that women were the stronger survivors.

One day the young women were given spades and told to dig up some ground to grow vegetables. It was as hard as rock, a back-breaking job. At the end of the day my hands were covered in blisters and I had accidentally cut into my foot with the spade. It left a nasty gash and with all the unhygienic conditions of the camp, the wound soon became septic. I was terrified that it would turn into an ulcer, for I had seen women lose a leg that way.

As children, we had often started a fire by catching the hot sun through a piece of glass. I knew where to find some broken glass and I got to work on my foot immediately, using the sun to literally burn away the flesh. It was extremely painful but it worked.

Needless to say the vegetable garden turned out to be a fiasco. It was a useless effort as nothing would grow in that barren ground, no matter how much we watered it. The few miserable shoots of cabbage that showed some promise, were ripped out long before they could reach their full growth.

If I were asked, 'What is the worst thing you remember about life in prison camp?' my answer would be the death that was always around us. Every day there was someone dying in the camp. A mother losing her baby, a child losing its mother. There was so much illness and misery, so little that could be done without proper medical equipment and medicine. Women and children both suffered from diarrhoea and dysentery, malaria and berri-berri, as a result of malnutrition. Every little scratch turned into a tropical ulcer. Children had worms and could not be treated. They stopped growing through lack of food and proper nutrition. And people just died from starvation.

Women had to drag themselves to roll call, no matter how sick they were. They would faint from standing for hours in the tropical sun. This was a favourite punishment of Nippon. The children stood on their mothers' feet because the ground was so hot it was scorching them. All the same, the women did not lose their sense of humour. We sang a lot while we were working because we knew that this annoyed the Japanese intensely. We also gave concerts to keep up our morale.

EVERY TIME I hear Beethoven's 'Minuet in G', it reminds me of a show we performed in camp, when I was dancing to this very melody. There was nothing better for keeping up our spirits than putting on a show or a concert, and while the Japanese did not really approve they did not stop us either. They used to like watching us from a distance, a change from the monotony of guarding the camp.

It was amazing to see the talent among the women but we could never have put on these shows if it were not for two very special ladies. They were spinsters and sisters, although you would never have thought so to look at them, for one was fat and the other thin. They had been teachers of music and physical education and among many other things they gave dancing lessons in the camp and formed a choir. We all admired them for their enthusiasm, patience, energy and organising talents.

On this particular occasion I was to dance an old-fashioned minuet with some of the other girls, dressed in my long blue flared dressing gown, with ribbons in my hair. It was a wonderful feeling just being able to dress up again. These two wonderful women helped us to cope with the boredom of camp life, pulling us through these most difficult times.

A SPECIAL convoy of Japanese arrived one day, in response to a dysentery epidemic in the camp. Another inspection, we thought. We were summoned to roll call in the compound. The visiting Japanese then handed each one of us a small cellophane bag. We were told that we had to fill the bag with our excrement and were given twenty minutes to perform this ridiculous task. We dispersed, roaring with laughter.

As soon as one of the women was lucky enough to produce something, she shouted out, 'Come here, have some of mine!'.

As most of us could not perform, we were only too glad to take up the offer, and so those who could shared with those who couldn't. After desperately trying for fifteen minutes, without result, I had a brain

57

wave, remembering the stray dog who used to find his way into our camp at night. Evidence of his visits were deposited in various places around the yard.

'Come with me', I called out to my friends, 'I know where to find some!'.

So in the end all our little bags were filled with faeces, one way or another. When the twenty minutes were up, we obediently handed our bags to the Japanese health visitors. They were very pleased. We were not surprised that we were never given the results!

This gift of love

THERE WAS a young woman in the camp who had no relatives with her. She was very much a loner. She was suffering from constant bleeding and we thought she may have cancer. I had heard it was her birthday and as she had not been at work duties for some time, I decided to look her up.

I found her lying in a dark corner on her mattress, a heap of misery and despair. She looked so ill, so pale, so thin. By her side was a bucketful of blood-soaked rags. She saw me looking at the bucket.

'I can't find anyone to wash them for me, and I am too weak to do it myself', she said, obviously feeling embarrassed.

'I'll wash them for you', I said. 'It can be my birthday present for you.'

My grandfather Henri O'Herne with his wife, Jeanne, and sister-in-law, in the buggy. The O'Herne children are in the background, with my father in the centre.

Henri and Jeanne with their children; (left to right) Edouard, Henri, Elodie and Célestin, my father.

A studio portrait of my mother, Josephine, in Holland,
taken by her father, a professional photographer.

My grandfather's house in the mountains at Bandoengan.

My mother and father at Tjepiering in 1923, with their first
three children; (left to right) Ward, myself and Aline.

My grandfather, Henri, Auntie Bets and my mother being conveyed across a river on sedan chairs.

'Our extended family', the household staff at Tjepiering; (left to right) Imah, Soemie, Sardie and Tjak.

The first 'edition' of children; (left to right) Ward, myself and Aline, c. 1929.

Tjepiering 1930. Henri O'Herne, a proud grandfather, nursing little Fien with (left to right) myself, Ward and Aline.

The O'Herne family at home in Tjepiering, 1938; (left to right) Ward, myself, my father, my mother, Fien, Céleste, Aline (and the dog called Hertha).

With my grandfather in the garden at Bandoengan.

Myself at the age of 16 in 1939.

Tom Ruff in Batavia, Java in 1945.

Tom and I with the jeep in Kramat camp, 1945.

Amsterdam, 1946. My family reunited; (left to right)
myself, my father, my mother, Aline. Céleste and Fien are
at the front.

Holland, 1946. 'Tom and I
wrote to each other every
day.'

Our wedding at 'St. Mary's the Mount' Catholic Church in
Walsall, England, August 14th 1946.

Tom and I with our first born daughter, Eileen,
in September 1949.

With my two daughters, Carol and Eileen, at the seaside,
Bridlington, 1954.

A family holiday in Bridlington in 1952.

Adelaide, South Australia, 1980. With Tom, my daughters
and grandchildren; (left to right) Eileen, Emma, Tom,
myself with Judd, and Carol.

Witnesses at the International Public Hearing in Tokyo, December 1992—all former 'comfort women' from North Korea, China, South Korea and the Philippines—with myself at right.

Embracing Wan Ai-Hua, 'comfort woman' from China, December 1992.

Tokyo, December 11th 1992. At the memorial shrine of the unknown soldier with former Japanese soldiers from World War II.

With my sisters, Céleste (left) and Fien (right) in Holland, August 1993.

'Would you really do that for me?' she said, her face lighting up.

From that day on I collected the bucket with the blood-soaked rags that she wore for protection, each day. I remember standing over this bucket with my head turned to one side because of the nauseating smell. Yet this gift of love filled my heart with great joy. The gratitude of this poor girl touched me and rewarded me a hundredfold.

Rumours were always spreading around the camp that the war was nearly over; that the Americans had landed; that Germany had lost the war, and so on. I think it was the rumours that helped to keep us going. But even more so were our communal prayers. Each evening we met in groups and prayed together — the rosary, novenas, or whatever was in our hearts. It was good therapy for the women for they could express their loneliness, fear, hurt and despair.

We prayed for the sick and for those who died, we prayed for our families and for each other, and we prayed for peace. I felt sorry for the women who had no religion and who could not pray. It was prayer that gave us strength and hope, and helped us to survive the war years.

In our camp we also had a number of old men, who were allowed to live in the women's camp because of their great age. One of these was Father Diderich, a Jesuit priest, formerly of the Ambarawa Parish Church. We all loved Father Diderich and his presence among us lifted our spirits and gave us security. However, he could not offer mass for us because he had no altar breads and wine.

One day Father Diderich recognised a boy's voice coming from the other side of the fence. Although he could not see the boy, he knew immediately that it was Atan, one of his former Indonesian altar boys.

'Is that you Atan?' Father Diderich whispered, standing close with his ear to the fence.

'Yes, it's me, Atan', the boy replied. 'I was hoping to find you Father.'

'Atan, listen carefully', Father Diderich continued. 'Can you smuggle some altar breads and wine from the sacristy into the camp?'

'Of course I can!' came the quick reply. Atan, being an altar boy, knew exactly where things were kept.

So they arranged to smuggle a small parcel of breads and wine through a hole in the fence. It had to be done at night, as soon as the night guard had passed a certain point. When Father Diderich received his precious parcel, he told us that we could celebrate Holy Mass. We did this, meeting secretly in small groups before dawn to stop the Japanese from finding out.

For quite some time we were able to have Sunday mass in this way and it was absolutely wonderful. I had never appreciated the full meaning and rich value of the mass until then. We prayed for the brave young altar boy who risked his life gladly each time he smuggled yet another parcel into our camp.

One night there was a lot of shouting and screaming by the fence. Atan had been caught in the act and dragged away by the guards. Some time later we heard that the boy had died of severe beatings from the Kempetai, the Japanese secret police. The church has many unsung saints and unknown martyrs. Atan is one of them. All my life I have remembered this brave Indonesian boy who gave his life so that we could receive Our Lord.

We tried to make Sunday a special day. Various denominations met within their own groups. Although we could no longer celebrate mass, we continued to come together with Father Diderich and listen to his talks, and to the readings and gospels of the day. For the first time in my life, the gospels took on a new meaning and I could understand them more clearly.

Father Diderich had the art of preaching and reading in a way that made you think he was talking especially to you. He explained the Gospel of Matthew 5: 1-12, the so called Beatitudes, or Sermon on the Mount. Suddenly these beautiful words of Christ's became a reality. Now I knew what it meant to be 'poor in spirit'. To be poor was not necessarily a negative thing. I was poor and stripped of everything, and yet I was rich because of it. It meant a total dependence on God for everything. We were in God's hands. I was aware of an inner strength that came from God and which would determine that I was going to survive all this hardship and suffering, no matter what!

The women of Kamp 6 were very fortunate to have a group of nuns living among them. I knew some of them, such as the nuns from the Ambarawa convent, and they included my former teacher, Sister Laetitia. In one of the barracks they had created their own little 'convent'. They continued to wear their habits, in spite of all the difficulties. Just to see the habits moving around the camp gave us hope and determination. Hard-working and always cheerful, the Sisters were our pillars of strength and they created a sense of peace in a world of misery.

In a way they were better equipped to deal with camp life than we were. They had taken their vow of poverty and were already poor, with no possessions that they could call their own. They did not have to worry about husbands or children, but gave all their energy to help and serve the women and children in our camp. They were the only ones respected by the Japanese.

Nothing was wasted

IT WAS our second Christmas in Ambarawa Camp and we had saved up rations for days to make sure we would have some sort of a Christmas dinner. I had found the branch of a tree and was wondering how I was going to turn it into a Christmas tree for Fien and Céleste. Imagine my luck when one of the Japanese casually threw away an empty cigarette packet. I hastily picked it up and looked inside. The packet was lined with silver paper.

Nothing was wasted from that discarded packet. I made a shiny star out of the silver paper and the cardboard was used for making the decorations. Late in the evening my mother and I were sitting outside. It was a beautiful still night and the dark sky was alive with flickering stars.

'Look, there's Venus', I whispered to my mother. My mother and father had made a pact that whenever Venus was visible in the sky, they would think of each other. I knew they were thinking of each other tonight and suddenly everything seemed so unreal. What had happened to our lives? What on earth were we doing here, locked away from the outside world? There seemed to be no future, no end to it all. What had happened to everything we had worked for, everything we once treasured?

I remembered my carefree, happy, childhood years. They seemed like a dream. Memories of climbing mango trees and swinging from the aerial roots of the Waringin tree, of playing in the warm rain and standing under the 'pantjoeran', the pipe that carried rainwater from the roof. I remembered the floor tiles in our house that felt so cool under my bare feet. The bathroom, or 'kamar mandi', with melatti flowers floating on the water, where I could splash the water

63

over my body with the 'gajong', or scooping pan. The safe feeling of sleeping under the netting of a 'klamboe'. The peaceful, undisturbed rest of the afternoon siesta. Relaxing on the verandah in the cane easy chairs, the iced drinks with long silver spoons and limes from the garden. People who were softly spoken and never in a hurry. The sound of the 'sapoe-lidi', or garden broom, as the gardener swept the driveway.

I was plunged back into reality when one of the women came out of our barracks to make the long trek to the latrines.

'Careful, I am carrying Tim's potty', she said, laughing as she passed us.

A potty was a treasured possession and a must for the elderly and the mothers with children. Those who entered the camp without one soon learned to improvise. Old saucepans and empty 'Blue Band' margarine tins were promoted to act as chamber pots. In the early hours of the morning you could witness a procession of women doing a balancing act with their chamber pots, trying not to spill one drop as they walked the long distance to the latrines.

February 1944

BY THIS time we had been interned in the Japanese P.O.W. camp at Ambarawa for almost two years. It was February 1944, hot and humid, seemingly just another day in our camp. The usual disturbances at roll-call, yet another death, the shouting of the guards, the crying of hungry children, the tempers of frustrated mothers, the heavy chores and duties of camp life.

That morning it had been my turn to empty the overflowing sewerage pits with the 'strontploeg', or 'shit brigade'. It meant emptying the sewerage pits with buckets, then carrying the buckets to a nearby stream to empty them out.

I had tied a large handkerchief over my mouth and nose, for the smell was unbearable. After an hour of performing this most unhygienic and loathsome task, I returned to the barracks with an aching back. My whole body, especially my hands, had a nauseating stench. I washed myself under a tap. It took quite some time to scrub the smell off my hands. If only I still had my piece of soap. Recently I had traded our last bit of soap for a couple of candles and some matches.

My little sister Céleste came running towards me when she saw me coming. She was crying. Her doll, her precious doll, was broken again.

'Please put her arm back on', she sobbed.

'I'll do it in a minute', I replied, as I threw myself onto the sleeping mat on the floor.

Suddenly there was a great commotion outside. I could hear the sound of Japanese army trucks and the excitement among the guards, signalling that some high ranking military had arrived for inspection, or the giving of new orders and rules.

A few days before, some Japanese military had

65

descended on the camp to take a register of all women, aged from seventeen to twenty-eight, taking names, ages and nationality. This had seemed like a warning sign and had caused great anxiety among the young girls.

As was common procedure with inspections, we were expecting to be summoned for roll call in the compound, while the Japanese guards searched through our pitiful possessions. However, this time the order was different.

All single girls, from seventeen years and up, were to line up in the compound at once. We were immediately suspicious. There was an uproar among the women, especially the mothers. Nervously, the girls ran towards their mothers and an air of fear rippled throughout our camp.

Our camp leader, Mrs Jildera, a strong and capable woman, angrily made her way to the office of the camp commandant, other women following close behind. They protested furiously against the order, at the same time trying to find out why only young girls had to line up. Mrs Jildera was rudely pushed aside and the order was repeated, this time sounding more alarming than before.

'That's you Jantje', my mother said, and I could hear the trembling in her voice, and see the fear in her eyes. I looked into our small mirror and pulled my hair across my face, trying to make myself look as unattractive as possible. Some girls tried to hide; one of them in the toilets. I could hear the shouting of the

Japanese as they marched towards the compound. I knew I had to obey orders, otherwise the whole camp would suffer.

Nervously, the young girls came forward, their anxious mothers close behind. We were assembled in a long line and I trembled with fear as a number of Japanese officers walked towards us.

I looked back to where my mother and sisters were standing. The thought of being parted from them made the tears stream down my cheeks. I did not like the look of these Japanese men. It was the way they looked us up and down, the way they laughed to each other and pointed at us. I stood there terrified, my head down, not daring to look up.

The Japanese officers paced up and down, up and down the line, inspecting each girl. Now they were standing directly in front of me. One of them lifted my chin with a stick so they could see my face. They stood there grinning, looking at my legs, at my face, at my body. Up and down they walked, sneering, pointing, laughing, while we girls stood frightened, heads down, not daring to look up or to look sideways at each other. More shouting as we were forced to look at our captors. Up and down they marched.

'Oh God,' I prayed, 'don't let them take me away, please don't let them take me away'.

After some discussion, half the girls were sent away. They ran towards their mothers and I could hear the relief as they safely reached their mothers' arms. I was left standing with a long line-up of girls,

67

while the Japanese continued looking, touching, pointing. Oh, how I wished I was ugly, or unattractive in some way. Again, some girls were sent back.

I was not sent away and the girls left standing automatically grasped each others hands. My whole body was numb with fear, my heart thumping. It was obvious by now that this was not just another inspection, or selection of a work party. We stood there motionless for what seemed like hours. We dared not look at one another, each one locked in her own fear. The selection process started all over again. This was to be the last one.

One officer seemed to be in charge. Ten girls were told to step forward; the others could go back to their anxious, waiting mothers. I was one of the ten. I could hear crying and wailing from the women as they tried to pull us back. They were fighting bravely, protesting loudly.

We had an interpreter in the camp, a pretty blonde Dutch woman who spoke fluent Japanese. She had been engaged to a Japanese businessman. Through the interpreter we were told to pack a small bag of belongings and report immediately to the camp office, where a truck was waiting to take us away.

We were not told any details, or where we were going. The girls and the mothers, and indeed, the whole camp, protested with all their might. The entire camp was pandemonium, with screaming, crying and protesting. Mrs Jildera, together with a party of nuns under the leadership of Sister Laetitia, stormed the office to protest and plead with the Japanese not to take the girls away. It was all in vain.

There was nothing anybody could do. Our human rights had been taken away, our freedom gone. Oppressed and bullied by the enemy, broken and enslaved helplessly by a brutal force, we were sheep for the slaughter.

The guards hurried us along and stood looking as we hastily packed a few things. My mother was nervously trying to find a suitable bag for me. I threw in my bible, prayer book, crucifix and rosary beads. At that moment they seemed the most important things. Almost like weapons, they would keep me safe and strong. My hands were shaking. I looked around the small, cramped living quarters that had been 'home' for my mother, Fien, Céleste and myself for almost two years. It seemed like a haven of safety to me now. My mother tried to be very brave but my two little sisters were crying, almost hysterical. I put my arms around them and hugged them, their tears wetting my cheeks. I loved them so much at that moment.

'I will come back', I said, trying to comfort them. 'I promise I'll be back soon.'

My mother and I could find no words to speak. We looked into one another's eyes and threw our arms around each other. There, in that moment, we both died in each other's arms. At least it seemed like dying. Would we ever see each other again? Where were they taking me? What would happen to me? All the fear was written on my mother's face.

69

I remember thinking that this must have been the same sort of fear Our Blessed Mother Mary suffered when she had her last meeting with her son, Jesus, before he was to die on Calvary. What sword of anguish must have pierced Mary's heart! This was the anguish and pain my mother was suffering when I was taken away from her. I felt an enormous compassion for the mother whom I had to leave behind.

The ten girls were now summoned together and flanked by guards, we were taken up to the front gate where the office and guardhouse stood. By now, all the women and children had rallied around, still stunned by what was taking place. How could this happen? How could they be so helpless, so beaten?

As we moved on, women tried to give us little gifts to take with us on our journey to the fearful unknown. I walked as if in a daze. One woman gave me a handkerchief, another gave me some quinine tablets. Father Diderich ran towards me.

'Here Jantje, take this', he said.

It was a small black book, a volume of the *Navolging van Christus — The Imitation of Christ —* by Thomas a Kempis. I still have this little book today and it is one of my dearest possessions.

Father Diderich looked at me so sadly, as if he knew what was going to happen to me. He clasped my hands as he handed me the small book, then gave me his blessing. I was never to see him again. Only a few months earlier, he had allowed me to make my one year temporary vows, the first step towards becoming a 'Religious'. From the moment I had told him that I wanted to become a nun, he had gently guided my soul and taught me how to meditate and detach myself from worldly things. He was moulding me into a bride of Christ and I had experienced a joy in my soul which I had never known before.

By this time all of us girls were crying. I tried to look for my mother and Fien and Céleste. There was so much more I wanted to say to them. Everything was happening very fast now. The high ranking Japanese were yelling out orders. More shouting, more pushing, more gestures to subdue us, as we were forced onto a big open truck.

Six other girls joined our miserable group. A total of sixteen girls were then taken from the Ambarawa camps, forced against their will. We huddled together like frightened animals, clutching our bags as a shield of safety. We had no idea where we would be taken. The gate of the camp was still open and I could see the weeping women and children waving, as my eyes tried to search out my mother and sisters. Suddenly I saw them in the crowd, then the gate closed. I burst out crying as the truck drove away.

I SOON realised that we were travelling on the main road from Ambarawa to Semarang, the capital of central Java. So many times I had travelled this same road with my family, for weekends or holidays with my grandfather, all of us singing happily in the car. It was the first time I had seen the

71

outside world since we had been taken prisoner in 1942. The countryside seemed changed somehow; the usual smiling faces of the Javanese were smiling no more. They looked poor, starving and frightened. As we came closer to the city of Semarang, we drove through the 'Heuvel terrein', Tjandi, the hillsides of Semarang. This had been considered the best area, as the hillsides were slightly cooler. I knew the area well and some of the houses were familiar. Many of my school friends had lived here and I had often spent weekends in their homes. Now the houses and gardens looked depressing as we drove past and memories went flooding through my mind.

The truck slowed down and pulled into the drive of a large Dutch colonial style house. The back of the truck was opened and seven girls were counted and told to get out. They were Lies, Gerda, Miep, Els, Annie, Betty and myself. I am using fictitious names here, for some of the girls still wish to remain anonymous.

There were more tears and goodbyes as the truck moved on with the rest of the girls. Immediately afterwards, the gates of the house were shut tight. I looked around and noticed with foreboding that the house and garden were completely surrounded by barbed wire and high fences. We were shoved towards the house. Heads down, we moved on, clinging onto our bags. I could hear the penetrating sound of male Japanese voices coming from the house.

The virgins' brothel

WE WERE soon to find out what sort of house we had been forced to live in. Nervously, we kept together as we were ushered in by the Japanese officer who seemed to be in charge. He looked sleazy, with a sardonic grin on his face. We mistrusted him immediately and became very suspicious. He took each girl to her own bedroom.

As I looked around my room I knew at once that this was a place to be feared, to be avoided. It had a double bed with a 'klamboe', or mosquito net, suspended above it. There was a marble-topped table, a mirror and a washbasin with a large matching jug. A towel rack, a wardrobe and a small table with two chairs completed the furnishings.

It did not take me long to unpack my small bag and hang my few dresses in the wardrobe. It smelt of mothballs and still had brown paper sheets lining the shelves. Looking through the window, I saw a large garden, several trees, and right at the bottom of the garden a fowl-pen.

The house itself was large enough to give each of us our own room. Like most Dutch homes in Java, there was also a very long L-shaped back verandah accommodating the kitchen, a store room for food, the servants' rooms, the bathroom, toilet and other spare rooms.

The house was named 'The House of the Seven Seas' by the Japanese. It still had the original furnishings from the Dutch family who had once lived here: ornaments of Delft Blue, a Dutch calendar showing the Edam cheese market — even a photo album of the happy, carefree family.

It made me feel intensely sad and I wondered who was now occupying our home in Tjepiering. Who was touching my things, staring at our photographs, using my hairbrush, eating from our plates?

That day we were given a good meal of 'nassi goreng'. It was the first decent meal we had seen since our internment but somehow we had no appetite, we were too scared to eat. An Indonesian 'baboe', or housemaid, and 'djongos', or houseboy, had brought in the food and nervously introduced themselves to us. Their names were Satinah and Hasan. They would do our various household chores: cooking, cleaning and washing. As I looked at them, I saw the only friends we would have. Their faces, looking back at me, were full of understanding, almost apologetic. Yes, they too knew what we all feared.

We were left more or less to ourselves on that first day and our whole conversation was about what was going to happen to us. Perhaps we would be sent out to work in a restaurant, or in a factory? There was still that faint hope.

That night we went to bed early but I could not sleep and neither could the other girls. We ended up in one big bed, huddled together in fear, too scared and shocked to talk. We just needed each other's company, desperately hoping that we would be safe if we stayed together. I suggested that we pray.

Opening my prayer book at random, it fell on
'Prayers of trust in God', Psalm 31, a trusting psalm
in times of ordeal. I read:

I come to you, Lord, for protection,
never let me be defeated.
You are a righteous God, save me, I pray!
Hear me, save me now!
Be my refuge, to protect me,
my defence, to save me.

For you are my rock, my fortress;
guide me and lead me as you have promised.
Keep me safe from the trap that has been set for me.
You are my shelter
I place myself in your care.
You will save me, Lord,
You are a faithful God.

Take pity on me, Lord,
because I am in trouble.
My eyes are tired from so much crying,
I am completely worn out.

But my trust is in you, Lord,
You are my God.
My days are in your hand, rescue me
from the hands of my enemies and persecutors.
Look on me with kindness
Save me because of your constant love!

I read the Psalm slowly, with tears in my throat.

The words gave us some comfort. Then we said 'The Lord's Prayer' together. Eventually, we fell asleep in each other's arms.

I WAS the first to wake up the next morning. Carefully I slid out of bed, trying not to wake the others, and tip-toed to my bedroom. Looking in the mirror, I saw my eyes were swollen from lack of sleep and all the crying. Suddenly, with this awareness, my whole body was locked into a feeling of intense fear. It was a feeling that from now on I would experience every day, every night.

I noticed that a glass jug with water, had been put on the table. 'Dear Satinah', I thought, as I removed the piece of net tulle that covered the jug, hearing the little beads that held it down tinkle as if trying to lift my spirits. The water tasted good on my dry lips. I was still wearing the dress from the night before as we had all got into bed fully clothed. My dress was wrinkled and creased and I looked forward to giving it to Satinah to be laundered. It would give me an excuse to talk to her and to Hasan.

While I was saying my morning prayers in my room, the house came alive with the voices of the other girls. Hasan served us a sober breakfast in the dining room and as we sat there around the table, we heard the sound of a motor vehicle, and of Japanese military boots moving around the house. We realised that from now on, our house was never going to be a private place and that the Japanese military would walk through, day or night, as they pleased.

Later that day, two more Dutch women arrived. They were married women, older than us, calling themselves Dolly and Yvonne. They seemed quite comfortable about being kept in the house. The first day of their arrival they kept very much to themselves. They told us they had volunteered to work in the house and our fears grew about the reason we had been brought to 'The House of the Seven Seas'.

The following day, some high ranking Japanese officers came to the house and we were all called to the living room. Communication with the Japanese was always difficult. The better educated or higher-ranking military would speak a little English and some of them had picked up enough of the local language to make themselves understood.

Somehow they made us understand that we were in the house for only one purpose. We were here for the sexual pleasure of the Japanese officers. We were here so that the Japanese military could have sex with us. We were to obey at all times and we were not allowed to leave the house, which was, in effect, a brothel. It was to be guarded at all times and trying to escape was useless. We had been enslaved into forced prostitution.

My whole body trembled with fear. My whole life was destroyed at that moment and collapsing under my feet. Not this, surely not this! My thoughts went to my mother and the safety of her embracing arms.

I wanted her so much at that moment and in a flash I could see her as the still centre of our loving family; of all that was good and pure and beautiful and safe.

The girls all stood there as if they had been struck by lightning. Then we started protesting loudly and with every gesture we could think of. We told them we would never allow this to happen to us, that it was against all human rights; that it was against the Geneva Convention and that we would rather die than allow it. The Japs stood there laughing at us.

'We are your captors', they told us. 'We can do with you what we like.'

We had already considered the possibility of escape. The house and grounds were well-guarded and anyway, as white women, we would be spotted and picked up instantly in the outside world.

The officer in charge produced some papers for us to sign. They were written in Japanese, which, of course, we could not read, but we had some faint idea of what they were about. We refused, we did not sign. Even though we were beaten and threatened and yelled at, we did not sign!

Soon after we saw the front verandah of the house being turned into a reception area where the Japanese could sit and talk and buy tickets for the girl of their choice. We were ordered to have our photographs taken. I put on my shabbiest dress. Once again we had to line up as one by one the photographer tried to make us smile. Instead the faces that stared back at him were defiantly angry, or sad.

Each of us was given a Japanese name, which was placed under our photograph on a pin-up board. I can't remember my name. I did not want to know about it. All I know is that it was the name of a flower. Flowers arrived at the house and each of us was given a vase of flowers to put in our bedrooms. Mine were white orchids. Instead of keeping them, much to the annoyance of the Japanese, we took the flowers and threw them into the garden, where they were consumed overnight by the snails.

A Japanese woman arrived on the scene. She had a hard face, was bow-legged and wore glasses. She looked rather clinical in her white uniform-style dress. We were all very pleased to see a woman in our house.

'At last, a woman!' I thought. 'Surely, a woman will understand us and help us and listen to our plight.'

But not this female. The Japanese war machine had turned her into a hard, cruel, ruthless woman. I asked her to please complain on our behalf to the highest authority, as we were being held in this brothel against our will. The woman showed no pity. She turned against me angrily, shouting as only the Japanese can.

IN THE meantime the whole house was being geared up to function as a brothel. In the bathroom, strange looking objects appeared. We had no idea what they were or how to use them. What we all dreaded most was now about to happen. Opening night had arrived.

We were told that we had to stay in our bedrooms after sundown. We were all so innocent. All of us were virgins and none of us knew anything about sex but we tried to find out from each other what to expect, what was going to happen to us.

Because we were virgins, prices were high on opening night. As soon as it began to get dark, we huddled together in the dining room around the table, terrified. Gerda, who was only eighteen years old, was almost hysterical with fear. I held her close in my arms to comfort her. Never before had I felt such paralysing fear, or felt so helplessly trapped. We sat there waiting, shaking, crying, holding each other close. By now, the fear had completely overpowered my body. Even to this day I shall never forget it, and in a way it has been there with me, all of my life.

I knew that the only thing that could help us now was prayer and in this the girls looked to me to lead them. I put my bible on the table and opened it at St Paul's letter to the Romans, Chapter 8. I read with trembling voice:

Let us find strength with the Lord. What we suffer in this life can never be compared to the glory which is waiting for us. We must share his sufferings if we are to share his glory. Nothing therefore can come between us and the love of Christ, even if we are troubled, or worried or being persecuted or hungry or naked, or being threatened by the sword or even attacked.

For your sake, says the scripture, we faced death at every moment, reckoned no better than sheep marked down for slaughter. These are the trials through which we triumph, by the power of him who loved us.

For I am certain of this: neither death nor life, no angel, or principalities or powers, nothing that exists, nothing still to come, no force whatsoever, neither the height above us nor the depth below us, nor any other created thing, will be able to separate us from the love of God, which comes to us in Jesus Christ our Lord.

The girls listened intently and I could sense that Christ was touching every one of them through these words of faith and love. The Psalms had always been a source of strength and comfort to me, so I turned to Psalm 27, and together we prayed those beautiful words:

The Lord is my light and my salvation, whom need I fear? The Lord is the fortress of my life, I will not be afraid.

We prayed the whole psalm, each verse giving us more consolation and we followed it by saying 'The Lord's Prayer'. The prayers had given us some calm. We crowded close together, holding each other's hands, needing each other's strength. We could hear the arrival of more and more military to the house; the throaty, ghastly sound of Japanese voices and

81

laughter, and boots treading the floor.

We were ordered each to go to our own rooms but we refused, staying close together, clinging to each other for safety. My whole body was burning up with fear, like electrical currents going through my arms and legs. It is a feeling I can't possibly describe, a feeling I shall never forget, never lose. Even after fifty years I still experience this feeling of total fear going through my body and through all my limbs, burning me up. It comes to me at the oddest moments. Sometimes when I see that it's getting dark, often while watching television, seeing an old war movie. I wake up with it in nightmares and can feel it just lying in bed at night.

The house was now filling up with Japanese military. We could sense their excitement, hear their laughter. We sat there waiting, huddled together till the time had come and the worst was to happen. Then they came.

Lies was the first girl to be dragged out of the dining room and into her bedroom. Then, one by one, the girls were taken, crying, protesting, screaming, kicking and fighting with all their might. This continued until all the girls were forcibly taken to their rooms.

After four girls had been taken, I hid under the dining room table. I could hear the crying coming from the bedrooms. I could feel my heart pounding with fear. I held tight to the wooden crucifix I had tucked into the belt round my waist. I had been wearing the crucifix like this continually, thinking that it might convey some message to the enemy and at the same time keep me strong. Eventually, I was found.

Sitting crouched up under the table, I saw the boots almost touching me. Then I was dragged out. A large, repulsive, fat, bald-headed Jap stood in front of me, looking down at me, grinning at me. I kicked him on the shin. He just stood there, laughing. He pulled me roughly by the arm. I tried to free myself from his grip but I could not. My fighting, kicking, crying, protesting, made no difference.

'Don't! Don't!' I screamed, and then in Indonesian, 'Djangan! Djangan!'.

He pulled me towards him and dragged me into the bedroom. I was fighting him all the time. Once in the bedroom he closed the door. I ran to a corner of the room, pleading with him in a mixture of English and Indonesian, trying to make him understand that I was here against my will and that he had no right to do this to me.

'Djangan! Djangan!' I repeated.

I stooped down and curled myself up in the corner like a hunted animal that could not escape from the hunter's net.

'Oh God, help me now!' I prayed. 'Please God, don't let this happen to me.'

The Jap stood there, looking down at me. He was in total control of the situation. He had paid a lot of money for opening night and he was obviously annoyed and becoming angry. He seemed very tall as I looked up at him from my crouched position. Taking his sword out of the scabbard, he pointed it at me, threatening me with it, yelling at me.

'I kill, I kill!' he shouted.

At that moment I really wanted to die. Dying was better than giving in to this man and being raped by him. Suddenly I was aware of an enormous strength filling me, a strength such as I had never known before. It was as if Christ himself was taking possession of my whole being, giving me the strength, taking over.

I told the Jap that he could kill me, that I was not afraid to die and that I would not give myself to him.

'Tidak, tidak — No, no.' I repeated it again and again.

He stood right over me now, pointing the sword at my body. I pleaded with him through my gestures, to allow me to say some prayers before I died. With his sword touching my flesh, I fell on my knees to pray. I think at that moment I loved God more than I had ever loved him, or anything, or anyone, ever before.

'My God, I love you, stay close to me now', I prayed. 'Dear Lord, forgive me all my sins. Jesus make me strong as I die for you. I love you Jesus, I love you with all my heart.'

A serene feeling of peace and calm came over me, as I was thus lost in prayer.

When I was eventually reunited with my mother,

she told me that at the same hour, on the same night, she was lying in bed and she suddenly saw a great light, a light that was almost blinding.

The Japanese officer was getting impatient now. He threw me on the bed and tore at my clothes, ripping them off. I lay there naked on the bed as he ran his sword slowly up and down, over my body. I could feel the cold steel touching my skin as he moved the sword across my throat and breasts, over my stomach and legs.

He played with me as a cat does with a helpless mouse. The game went on for a while and then he started to undress. I realised then that he had no intention of killing me. I would have been no good to him dead. He threw himself on top of me, pinning me down under his heavy body. I tried to fight him off. I kicked him, I scratched him but he was too strong. The tears were streaming down my face as he raped me. It seemed as if he would never stop.

I can find no words to describe this most inhuman and brutal rape. To me, it was worse than dying. My whole body was shaking. I was in a state of shock. I felt cold and numb and I hid my face in the pillow until, eventually, I heard him leave.

As soon as he had gone, I gathered what was left of my clothing and ran to the bathroom, feeling that if only I could wash everything away from my body it would be all right. In the bathroom, I found the other girls all crying, all trying to do the same thing. Trying to wash away all the dirt, the shame, the hurt, as if we could wash away all that had happened to us.

Where were we to go now? I dared not go back to the dining room or the bedroom, so I decided to hide myself. As quietly as possible, I left the bathroom and hid in a room on the back verandah. My heart was pounding furiously in my body. My whole body was shaking with fear.

'Oh God, don't let anybody find me!' I prayed. 'Not again, I can't go through it again.'

Waiting there in the darkness, I could hear excitement outside. All the girls were hiding somewhere in the house or in the garden, and the Japanese were trying to find us. Things were not going as they had planned.

After a while, the angry voices and the sound of heavy army boots came closer and I was dragged out of my hiding place. The night was only young; it was not yet over. There were more Japanese waiting. The terror started all over again.

This was only the beginning of what we had to endure from now on. I had never realised that suffering could be as intense as this. I offered it all up to Jesus Christ and to make up to God for all the sins committed by the Japanese. But I asked myself how I was to survive the days, the months to follow.

AT THE end of that first, horrific opening night, in the early hours of the morning, seven frightened, exhausted girls huddled together to cry over lost virginity and to give each other comfort and strength.

How many times was each one raped that night? What could we do?

In the morning, Hasan served us some breakfast. He seemed very shy and mumbled something to say how sorry he was about last night and about what had happened to us. Just as we were about to leave the table, Dolly and Yvonne, the 'volunteers', as we called them, came in. They seemed to be in good spirits. I was curious to know why they had actually volunteered to work in a brothel as prostitutes for the Japanese. As soon as I got the chance, I asked them. Their answer was simple and to the point.

When some young girls had been taken out of their prison camp, two of them only sixteen years old, Dolly and Yvonne felt sorry for them and suggested to the Japanese that they could go in their place.

'Anyway', added Dolly, 'I have no intention of dying of starvation. I want to get out of this war alive.'

My thoughts went to the two young girls who were spared because of Dolly and Yvonne. I learned a very important lesson that day — never to judge people!

Back in my bedroom I found Satinah changing the bed linen. She looked at me sadly, and I could see tears in her dark brown eyes. She wiped them away with the end of her faded 'kebaya' sleeve. I went over to her and put my arms around her, hugging her. Thus we comforted each other. I wanted so much to talk to her. She reminded me of Imah and Soemie, whom I had loved so dearly as part of our family in

Tjepiering. I asked her about herself as we sat there on the bed. She had worked in the household of a Dutch family in a house not far from here.

'Those were happy times', she told me, 'when we had plenty of food and work. Now I cannot even buy myself a new 'kebaya' or give my children proper food.'

Indeed, the Indonesian people had suffered greatly under Nippon.

Lies came into my bedroom, her rosary beads dangling from her hands. She was the only other Catholic girl among the seven; the others shared a Protestant upbringing.

'Shall we?' she asked, holding up her beads.

From that day on, Lies and I prayed our rosary together, each morning, sometimes more than once. It was amazing how sharing the rosary could have such a healing effect on us. When I was reunited with her fifty years later, in Holland, the first thing she said was, 'Remember all the rosaries we prayed!'.

The handkerchief

IN THE daytime, we were supposed to be safe, although the house was always full of Japanese, coming and going, socialising, eyeing us up and down. There was little privacy and consequently we were often raped in the day as well. But my fear was worse for the evening to come. As it was getting dark, it would gradually build inside me until finally it was burning up my whole body.

Each evening before the house was 'opened', I hid in a different place, but I was always found and I soon ran out of hiding places. In desperation, looking for somewhere new, I climbed a large tree, right in the corner of the back garden. I had always been good at climbing fruit trees as a child so I had no difficulty in getting myself high up, where I sat, sheltered among the branches and leaves.

After a while, I was aware that everybody was looking for me. They must have looked in all the usual places and were now impatient, angry and shouting loudly. My heart was pounding as I tried to keep as quiet as possible.

Now they were looking outside as they thought I might have escaped. I sat up in that tree for at least thirty minutes, glad in the knowledge that it had saved me one rape. Finally, someone came with a torch and I knew then that my luck had run out.

The torch was shining up the tree, right into my face. The game was up and the Japanese were furious. I received a terrible beating as punishment and then was dragged into the bedroom where another Jap was already waiting for me. The beating had been worth it. I learned that every minute, every bit of time that could be salvaged, helped to delay the horrifying start of the evening.

As time went on we discussed our situation obsessively, trying to work out how best we could deal with it. We shared our fear, our pain and our humiliation. Sometimes we tried to be young again and laugh a little, and talk about pre-war days. We needed each other desperately and so a bond of friendship and love formed between us, giving us tremendous support. The girls turned to me for spiritual strength and each day I led them in prayer and read from the Psalms and the Gospels. I still wore the wooden crucifix, tucked into my belt and found that the Japanese called me 'the girl with the cross'.

I took out the white handkerchief that one of the women had pushed into my hand the day we were taken from the Ambarawa camp. One morning when we were gathered together on the back verandah, I got out a pencil and asked each girl to write her name there. Then I wrote in the centre, 26-2-'44, the date we had been forcibly removed from the camp. Afterwards, I embroidered over the writing, each name a different colour. I kept this white handkerchief with the seven names on it hidden for fifty years, afraid that my family would ask me, 'What do the names on this hankie mean?'. It has been one of my dearest possessions but also my most hidden, the secret evidence of the brutal crimes that had been done to us.

The Haircut

I WAS living in constant fear, a fear so terrible that my whole body was consumed by it. I was crazy with fear. It was with me every moment of the day and the night. I was getting desperate. I had tried everything I could think of to prevent myself being raped. One morning I found myself asking the question, 'What else can I do?'.

I looked in the mirror. There was only one thing left. I could make myself so repulsive that it would revolt the Japanese. There was a pair of scissors in the dressing table drawer, so I sat in front of the mirror that morning and I cut off all my hair. I hacked away at it until I was quite bald. I had cut it very close to the scalp and it was uneven. I looked really terrible.

I stared at my blank, empty face in the mirror.

'I want to look ugly', I thought. 'Then they won't want me.'

When the other girls found me like this they were horrified.

'Jannie, what have you done?' cried Gerda, the first one to see me.

Els quickly got a scarf to cover my baldness but I refused to put it on. I wanted to be bald and ugly.

'Jannie, if it helps, then I will cut off my hair too', said Lies, to support me.

I kept my head uncovered and the rumour spread that one of the girls had cut off all her hair in order to be as unattractive as possible. It turned me into a sight-seeing object. Everyone wanted to know the girl who had cut off her hair. So my attempt to repel the Japanese had perversely drawn their attention even more.

Playing for time

THE JAPS enjoyed playing card games and we used packets of cards from the house to hold off the inevitable rape. Each encounter followed a bizarre routine. First, I tried to make them understand that I was in this house against my will, that I had been forced into this and I would not allow them to touch me. This plea never made the slightest difference. It brought only sarcastic laughter. The next strategy was to buy time, any pretext would do, and this was when the card games were useful. Every minute, every half-hour that I could hold off being raped was important, because as soon as one Jap was finished, another would be waiting.

When they got tired of this, they would suddenly show impatience, throw the cards across the table and grunt some language I could not understand. Then they tried to get me on the bed.

Always, each and every time, I tried to fight them off. To me it would have been a mortal sin not to fight. Never once did any Japanese rape me without a violent struggle. Often they threatened me with death. Perhaps it would have been easier not to keep fighting as the Japs always won anyway. But I could never do this. During these fights I hit out strongly and delivered some mighty blows and kicks and scratches. Quite often I injured the Japanese and because of this, because of my persistent fighting, I was called into the office and told that if I did not stop they would move me to a brothel downtown for soldiers — a brothel with native girls. There, the conditions were worse and I would have to 'work' during the day as well as at night. I left the room panic-stricken, tears rolling down my face. I felt so utterly helpless, so tired, so worn out.

As I walked past Miep's room, I suddenly felt an urge to see her. I knocked at the door but there was no answer. The door was slightly ajar and as I pushed it open, I saw her lying on the floor, blood stains all over her dress. Her face was so white. I called out for help. She had always seemed to be the strongest and the wisest of us girls. We had so often listened to her advice. But for Miep, the cup had overflowed. She had cut her wrists in an effort to take her own life. I had arrived just in time.

Our Japanese woman guard showed her efficiency as a nurse. Miep was bandaged up and driven off to hospital. When she came back a few days later, she didn't say much and we did not really talk about it, but we gave her more of our support and love.

Although Dolly and Yvonne were keeping to themselves, we were sometimes glad of their presence. A reputedly brutal and much-feared Japanese arrived at my room one evening. I panicked the moment I saw him and ran from the room. Yvonne saw the state I was in.

'Here, leave him to me', she said kindly. 'I'll take this one for you.'

She played up to the 'bastaard' as we called him and lured him into her own bedroom. Yvonne had Belgian blood and she spoke with a faint French-Flemish accent. I liked her. She was the more good-hearted of the two, helping me a number of times when I was looking for a hiding place.

'Come and hide under my bed', she would whisper. 'You should be safe there.'

And so I did and found myself an embarrassed but grateful witness to Yvonne's love-making with her customers.

'You'd better get out now,' she'd say after some time, 'before you get into any trouble.'

There came a morning when a Japanese doctor arrived at 'The House of the Seven Seas'. Immediately I thought that he would be able to help us. Surely as a doctor he would have compassion for us. I asked to speak to him and went to see him in his office. Making my entrance with the usual polite bow, I tried to explain what was happening — that we were here against our will, that we had been taken out of the prison camp by force, that this was against the Geneva Convention and could he please report this scandalous crime to higher authorities.

The doctor looked at me with his hands folded behind his head, leaning back in his chair and eyeing me up and down. He showed no interest in what I had told him and no signs of compassion or apology. My heart sank, but at least I had tried. He stood up briskly now and walked towards me but I was too quick for him as he tried to grab me. I dashed out of the room and into the back garden to hide myself.

I made for the fowl pen which was small and rather low. He was big and fat and would not be able to follow me. I crouched down among the chickens, under the loud cackling and the flying of feathers. A few minutes later a big fat panting torso tried to squeeze through the narrow opening of the pen, accompanied by hideous laughter from onlookers. As always, I was the loser in the end. The doctor brutally raped me on this, his first visit to the house.

IN THE days leading up to subsequent visits, gynae-cological equipment was installed in one of the rooms on the back verandah. This was to be the room where from now on we would be examined for any possible venereal disease.

The morning arrived when this was to begin. To give each other support, one girl accompanied an-other during the examination. I was terrified and felt totally humiliated by this Japanese doctor examining me in this way. He visited our house regularly and each time he raped me during the daytime, as if it were a part of the process.

There was no door to the examination room and to make things worse, and to humiliate us even further, there were always other Japanese men looking on. They were encouraged to come into the room or stand in the open doorway and look at us while we were being examined. These examinations became just as horrific as the rapes.

This humiliation was as much as I could stand. For the first time in my life I fully understood what Jesus must have suffered when he was stripped of his garments before crucifixion. Each time, after the doctor's visit, I went to my room and prayed the Tenth Station of the Cross — Jesus is stripped of his garments.

Arrived at last at the place of sacrifice, they prepare to crucify him. His garments are torn from his bleeding body, and he, the Holy of Holies, stands exposed to the vulgar gaze of the rude and scoffing multitude.

'Dear Lord,' I prayed, 'They can strip me of everything. They can take everything away from me, humiliate me, abuse me and ruin my young life. They can take away my youth, my freedom, my possessions, my family, my self-esteem, my dignity, but they can never take away my love for you. They can never take away my faith. This is mine, my most precious possession and nobody, nobody can take it away from me.'

With the prophet Isaiah, 38:15, I prayed, 'I will give glory to you all the years of my life for my sufferings.'

Night and day I am with you

IN ALL these wartime years of Japanese occupation in the Netherlands East Indies, I only met one decent Japanese. This man gave me a short breathing space during these terrible months of suffering.

My elder sister, Aline, was still living in Semarang, her services with the Netherlands Indies Railways (N.I.S.) still valued by the Japanese. Along with a small number of Europeans — German, French and Dutch — she was not interned. But it was just as hard for these people to survive outside the camp as it was for us on the inside. At a later stage, all were imprisoned.

One day I asked our home-help, Hasan, if he would do me a great favour and take a letter to my sister in town — or rather would he be prepared to smuggle the letter out. If he was found doing this, it could mean death. He said he would take the letter to Aline because he felt so sorry for the 'nonni blanda', the European girl. He wanted to help me in some way and he was willing to take the risk. I thanked Hasan for this most courageous and loving deed and told him that my sister would reward him handsomely. His face wrinkled up in a great smile.

Aline was devastated by the news in my letter and the atrocities that had been done to me and she began to conceive a plan to help me. She shared a house with a German couple. The husband was a doctor. Aline had worked as a nurse with the Red Cross and often helped him when the need arose. She had also come to know a number of Japanese during her time with the N.I.S. and while working with the doctor. Who could she turn to now? Could she trust any Japanese at all?

She turned to a man called Yodi, a Japanese whom she sensed she could trust. He was genuinely upset when she told him my story and said that he was prepared to help me. They planned that Yodi would visit the brothel and 'buy' me out for the whole night, thereby preventing any other Japanese from raping me while he was there. Once again with the help of Hasan, I received a letter from my sister.

Hasan was excited when he handed me the letter and showed me the gifts that Aline had given him. He told me that my sister looked very much like me and that she was a very kind lady. I cried with joy when I saw Aline's handwriting and before opening the envelope, I pressed it lovingly to my heart. She was suddenly so close, and yet so far — such a short distance but still I could not reach her. But now she shared my suffering and that was a tremendous comfort to me. In her letter, she told me to expect a visit from Yodi.

Hasan also gave me a small parcel from Aline, which he had concealed under his clothing. It contained medicine, quinine tablets, a piece of soap — very precious at that time — and a Sunday Missal. On the front-page she had written a poem called 'De roeping tot het kruis van Christus' — 'The Call to the Cross of Christ'.

She also wrote on the next page in Dutch, 'Night and day I am with you. With all my thoughts and strength, I beseech God to help us.'

I still have this missal today. It brought comfort and strength during those dark war years and so I will treasure it always.

That evening, a friendly looking, slightly built Japanese man came looking for me. I immediately knew he was Yodi, the one who was going to help me and my heart suddenly jumped for joy. All the fear seemed to be released from my body. I asked him to come to my bedroom and he followed me, looking shy and awkward, while I regarded him as the saviour of the world.

He was so understanding and so ashamed at what the Japanese had done to us. Apologising with humble gestures, he told me that I had nothing to fear and showed me the ticket he had bought for the whole night.

We talked for a while. It still amazes me how we managed to communicate, but we did, with a bit of this language and a bit of that, along with plenty of gestures and the art of drawing.

'Thank God for the cards', I thought, for I had been wondering what I was going to do with him all evening.

I taught him Dutch card games and he showed me some Japanese ones, and of course, I tried to convert him to Catholicism! I had not had a good night's sleep for so long and I thanked God that tonight I was going to sleep peacefully. When the time came, I offered Yodi to sleep on my bed and that I would sleep on the floor but he insisted that he would do this.

For a week, he came to the house every night to keep me safe. To pass the time, I thought of all the childhood games we could play where language is not a barrier, and so we played noughts and crosses and other games where drawing was the basis.

This short period of Yodi's visits could not last. He told me he was being teased and laughed at by his Japanese friends because he visited the brothel every night and stayed all night. It must have been very hard on him, especially as he never once touched me.

During the time of his visits he often gave me letters from Aline and small parcels my sister had made up for the other girls. Lies, too, had found someone who, for a short period of time, was able to help her. This Japanese man was a Christian and had lived in America for a while. He felt sorry for Lies and was able to visit her several times to keep her free from being raped.

My trust in God was great

AFTER YODI had helped me for two weeks, his visits suddenly stopped. I asked Hasan once more to visit my sister. Aline replied that Yodi was moving out of Semarang with other troops and that he was not coming again. Although I had always thanked him in the mornings for keeping me safe during the night, I felt sorry that I never had the chance to say goodbye, and to thank him again for all he had done for me.

As the months passed, all of us girls lost weight. We barely touched our food, even though Satinah tried to tempt us with her cooking. I don't know what we would have done without Hasan and Satinah and their love and support. They were always there with a smile, or ready to help us to hide. Countless times did Satinah hide us in her room, countless times did Hasan point the wrong way when the Japanese were looking for us. All of us were exhausted, our nerves stretched to the limit. Continually, we put in protests to any high ranking officer who visited the house, but they always fell on deaf ears.

Each of us had to find her own way of dealing with the situation, trying to keep up strength and hope at the same time. My inner strength came from my faith, from prayer and from God. I never said to

God, 'Why did this happen to me? Why me, Lord?'. I knew that it must all be in God's plan, and everything that happened only strengthened my faith. When I had nothing left, when everything had been taken from me, there was only God and me, and so I needed God more than ever before. It gave me the feeling that I totally depended on God alone and this knowledge brought me very close to him, a thing that doesn't easily happen in life. But it did happen for me under these circumstances.

I missed my mother and my two young sisters terribly. My mother was in poor health and very weak when I had to leave her. I worried in case she died. How would Fien and Céleste manage without her? But my trust in God was great and somehow I knew that I would see them again. Countless times, in my imagination, I pictured the scene of my mother and father being reunited, and our family being whole again. It was this dream of family love and the goodness I had known that kept me going. My happy family life and secure childhood gave me the base on which to survive all this suffering.

More anxiety came my way when I thought I was pregnant. I was terrified and almost sure it was the result of that first night. Not this, not this as well! How could I expect to give birth to and love a child conceived in such horror. My mind could hardly comprehend the situation. As always, I put my life into God's hands, knowing that whatever happened to me was his plan, working itself out in my life. He would never abandon me.

That morning after breakfast, I told the other girls. I could see by their faces that they were as shocked as I was. There was always the fear of falling pregnant, just as there was the fear of venereal disease. The Japanese were supposed to wear protection but many did not bother.

Offering me their strength and their love, the girls gave me the opportunity to talk about it. Their advice was to tell our much dreaded Japanese woman guard. There might just be a chance that they would let me go back to the prison camp if I was pregnant.

I approached the woman in the office, where she was always counting money at this time of the morning. She looked at me angrily, for disturbing her. I had bowed respectfully on entering the room but she made me bow again, deeper this time. It was not too difficult to explain the situation and as an answer to the problem, she produced a bottle of tablets, giving me a handful to swallow. I did not know what kind of tablets they were but obviously they were intended to induce a miscarriage. I shook my head and refused to swallow them. I could not kill a foetus, not even this one. It would be a mortal sin if I did. I continued to refuse them but eventually the tablets were forced down my throat and I miscarried shortly afterwards.

THERE WERE some cane easy chairs on the back verandah and if we ever got the chance, this is where we would sit and talk, always, instinctively, as far away from the bedrooms as possible. Overhearing our conversation, Dolly and Yvonne joined us one morning, something they did not often do.

'Can I give you some advice?' Dolly said. 'You must get yourselves a 'tjinta', or lover. Pick out a few Japanese men that you know are not going to give you too hard a time. Play up to them, encourage them, so that they will come back each night. It's better to have these same men each night than different ones. Really, you will make it much easier for yourselves this way.'

I remembered seeing Dolly and Yvonne flirting with some of the Japs, laughing and joking as if it was all a game of fun and pleasure. It used to repulse me. I knew that even if this advice was wise, I could never follow it.

HOW LONG were we in the Semarang brothel? I can't remember exactly, but it was at least three months. More and more military visited the house in the daytime so that now even those precious hours were not our own. How much longer could we go on, we asked ourselves. The systematic rapes were showing their effects on us.

As I sat on the verandah one twilight, Hasan seemed to appear from nowhere to turn on the lights. He had this soft way of moving about on his bare feet.

'Thank you Hasan', I said, as I listened to the cicadas who had started their monotonous shrill song. The 'tjitjaks', the small lizards, attracted by the light, immediately came out of their hiding places, darting across the wall. A few friendly toads hopped on the verandah to join in the singing and the hunt for insects. All these were signs of the approaching evening. I had grown up with these beautiful sounds as a child but now they brought on the inevitable fear until my whole body was consumed by it.

I was looking at the drawings in my lap. I had made some pencil sketches of Lies, Gerda, Miep, Els, Betty and Annie. I wanted to remember these girls for always, and not only by their names embroidered on the handkerchief. The friendship and bond between us was a great treasure. Now, I had their portraits and I was pleased with the result. Each girl had touched my life in a special way. Each girl had something special to offer to the whole group and now, each of us was tired out.

Lies and I prayed more and more rosaries. Gerda was a bundle of nerves and crying more than ever. Miep walked around the place as if in a coma. Betty was endlessly crocheting little mats to soothe her nerves, while Els and Annie exchanged numerous recipes, using their love of food and cooking to distract them.

We had a number of visits from high ranking military and there were long discussions in the office, accompanied by much shouting. Suddenly the order came that we were to pack up our things to leave. No reasons were given. We were not told where we were going and we were terrified. I wrote a hasty letter for Hasan to give to Aline.

What did they have in mind for us? Would we end up in a worse situation than we were in now? Were we going to another brothel? We knew there were several more brothels with Dutch girls in Semarang.

There were lots of tears when we had to say goodbye to Hasan and Satinah. We had come to love these dear people and it broke our hearts to leave them behind. Once again a frightened group of young girls was trucked away, this time to make a long train journey, lasting two days.

From the time we left Semarang Station all the windows on the trains were boarded up. The conditions on the train were disgusting and we could not see where we were going. The ride was exhausting, with none of us able to sleep. It took us to Bogor, 33 miles south of Batavia, in West Java and we ended up in Bogor Camp.

The Japanese gave us no explanation why our stay at the Semarang brothel had suddenly ended. All we knew was that we were back in another prison camp. Our time of working in a Japanese brothel was over.

Part 3

Bogor Camp

AS SOON as we arrived at the Bogor prison camp, the Japanese told us that we were never to tell anybody, ever, of what had happened to us. If we did, we would be killed, along with our families. The silence began then and there, the silence that was forced upon us.

The camp in Bogor was to be a transit camp only. It consisted of a number of former Dutch homes, fenced off completely and turned into a prison camp. Here, we were brought together with all the other Dutch women who had been forcibly taken out of their camps and made to work in brothels for the Japanese. Now, for the first time, in Bogor, we could see the enormity of this monstrous crime against human rights. There were over one hundred Dutch women in the camp, all war rape victims of the Japanese military.

In the meanwhile, our mothers and their children were also put on trains and were making the two-day journey to Bogor and so we were reunited with our beloved families. It was a moment of sheer rejoicing when I spotted my mother and Fien and Céleste among the new arrivals.

We clung to each other for a long while as if we never again wanted to let go. We cried tears of joy and stood, just looking at one another. My mother's appearance was terrible. She had lost more weight and her hair was almost white now. There were dark rings under her eyes that showed the signs of worry and strain. Céleste, as always, was clinging onto her doll. I was surprised to see, however, that it was not her favourite doll, Jolanda.

'Where is Jolanda?' I asked.

'I'll tell you later', was my mother's quick reply.

It was the only time the war had got the better of our dear mother. It seems that when they were packing up to leave the Ambarawa camp, she refused to let Céleste pack her beloved Jolanda in her backpack. Céleste cried and argued and tried to explain that Jolanda was not too big and too old, but mother said she had 'lost' Jolanda. Céleste understood and had completely forgiven mother, long before she had grown up. But our dear mother never forgave herself and could not bear, ever, to talk about it.

Fien, who had always been a shrewd child, looked at me with a curious expression. She had noticed the scarf around my head and I realised that I had some explaining to do.

'I will soon be able to start up school again for you', I said to distract her attention.

This seemed to cheer them up and I took them to the house that had been allotted to us. Even though we had to share it with others, it seemed sheer luxury to have this house for our living quarters after the cramped conditions of the Ambarawa Camp. Again, there was still some furniture in the house and a few possessions of the Dutch family who had once lived there happily.

From papers, we found that the name of the family was Pley. We got to know something about them from photographs still in the house. We used their plates, one of which I still have. We used their cutlery and cut our nails with 'Mr Pley's nail scissors', as we called them. Most Dutch homes had been looted after the Dutch citizens had been interned, except for the homes that had been occupied by the Japanese.

The time we spent in Bogor Camp probably saved my mother's life, as we were given some better food. This really surprised us and it almost seemed as if the Japanese wanted to make up for all the abuse that had been done to us.

We went to bed early on that first night. Fien and Céleste were exhausted after the long train journey and they were soon sound asleep. A feeling of immense safety came over me as we were lying there, side by side in the dark, all together again. I snuggled close into the hollow of my mother's arm. I was not yet able to tell her all that had happened to me but I did not really have to. It was as if she already knew. That night, in the dark, she kept on stroking her fingers over my bald head, and softly and lovingly, full of understanding, my mother's fingers soothed my head until I fell asleep.

The next day, finding a moment alone with her, I told her all that had happened to me. I only ever talked about it just this once. I could see that she could not cope with it and so we never talked about it again, and again the silence deepened.

It was the same with the other girls. They could never really talk to their mothers about it either, for the mothers were too devastated. While we had been in the brothel, we girls were able to talk to each other. Now, there was only silence.

We had no counselling, no help from anyone. We just had to carry on as if nothing had happened. I knew that it was extremely difficult for my mother to cope with all the emotions she felt at that time. I was her daughter. This had happened to her daughter! I wanted to show her and my two young sisters that I was still the same Jan, that I had not changed, that I still had the same joy as always, and that we could laugh together again. From now on I covered my head with a scarf and many of my friends rallied round and gave me pieces of cloth to wear over my bald head.

The following morning, the call of 'tenko', or roll call, made me realise that nothing had changed. We were still prisoners of the Japanese. We were still in prison camp and left to the whims and mercy of yet another camp commandant. This one had a moustache and was immediately given the nickname, 'de snor', meaning 'the moustache'. He had the same mean, ruthless look about him that I now associated with all Japanese.

This first roll call in Bogor Camp is forever engraved in my memory. We had all lined up and dutifully made our required ritual, bowing deeply. We were a pitiful row of abused girls, grief-stricken mothers and tired children as we stood there, waiting in the sun.

As we were being counted, the commandant noticed me. He must have heard the story about the girl from the 'Shoko', or officers club, 'comfort station', who had cut off all her hair. He stood directly in front of me, curious, wanting to know what was under the scarf. With an enraged voice, he ordered me to step forward. As I did so, I could feel my mother behind me, trying to pull me back in an instinctive effort to protect me. All the women gasped, while some of them quickly pulled my mother back into line. They were afraid that she would be beaten. I stood there, frozen with fear.

The commandant whisked his sword out of its sheath. Then, with a quick flick of the sword, he removed the scarf from my head. There I stood, bald-headed, humiliated in front of the women, the children and the Japanese guards, an object of scorn, a witness to the brutal abuse that had been done to me. My two sisters tell me that even to this day, they will never forget that moment when the camp commandant ripped the scarf off to see my bald head, wanting to make sure that the rumours he had heard were true.

In the Bogor Camp we were able to buy a few extras if we had any money — vegetables, rice, an egg, bananas, oil. This trading was done through the guards, who were only too happy to make some extra money. We were not supposed to have any money left but somehow the women were able to produce it and exchange it for Nippon money. I remember my mother exchanging her last Dutch golden coin of 10 guilders, and receiving 299 Nippon 'roepiah' for it.

We never wasted anything that could possibly be eaten. The banana skins were fried in the oil, the egg shells were crushed to serve as calcium intake.

Within no time I had a school for the children running again and we had work parties organised for the running of the camp. This new order was interrupted by a terrible incident during those first few weeks. One of the Japanese guards entered the house of one of the women at night. At first he made out that he had come for a chat and to do some trading. Then, suddenly, he turned on her and tried to rape her. Obviously he knew where we had come from and must have thought we were an easy target. There followed a lot of screaming and shouting and uproar and the soldier disappeared into the night.

The incident of this attempted rape was immediately reported to the camp commandant. At morning roll call, one of the Japanese guards was called and ordered to stand in the centre of the compound. The commandant marched up to him and dressed him down severely in a language we could not understand.

The guard stood there, terrified. The commandant then took out his revolver and handed it to the

113

guard. The poor man was then forced to shoot himself through the mouth.

All this was witnessed by the women and children. Horrified as we were, we at least knew that we were safe from rape in future. But we could not help pondering what a strange mentality the Japanese had. A short while ago we had been raped by at least ten Japanese a day, with the approval of the Japanese Emperor, Hirohito, the Kempeitai, and the highest military authorities. Now this man was forced to shoot himself for trying to do exactly the same thing.

Apart from this incident, the time in Bogor was too good to last. During those few months my mother put on a little weight before once more we were transported to another camp, just at a time when our vegetable garden was showing some promise. Always this fear of what now? Where will we be going this time? This was to be our last move. We were sent to a large women's prison camp called Kramat, in Batavia, now known as Jarkata.

Hoeren Camp

ON ARRIVAL at Kramat, we found that our quarters were completely isolated from the rest of the camp. We were, in fact, in a camp within a camp. The Japanese officers were afraid that rumours would spread and that the truth would be uncovered of what had been done to us. By isolating us, they tried to prevent the terrible story from leaking out. Again, we were ordered never to tell anyone about the atrocities, on pain of death.

Our humiliations and sufferings had still not come to an end. The women in the other part of Kramat Camp had been ordered not to make contact with us. Somehow, rumours still spread as to why we were being kept in isolation and cruelly, they gave our camp the name 'Hoeren Camp', meaning 'Camp of Whores'. They thought we had been voluntary workers in brothels for the Japanese. They also believed that because of this we were being given special treatment and food. None of it was true. Our food was worse than ever before and we were starving just as much as all the other women and children in Kramat.

Conditions there were much worse than at Ambarawa, and those had been bad enough. At times, the women from the other part of the camp would shout abusive names at us through the fence and throw messages, written on paper and tied to a stone, over the fence. They addressed us as whores and traitors, or 'konynen', meaning 'rabbits'. The only women who believed our stories were the Catholic nuns, with whom I had secretly made contact.

One of the women in our camp was nicknamed 'Blondie' because of her fair complexion and blonde hair. Blondie had been a volunteer worker in a brothel, and had been returned to the camp, pregnant. She had no idea who the father was, only that it had been the result of her time in the brothel.

Blondie was a nice young woman, very joyful, and even proud of her pregnancy. The children liked her and as her stomach grew larger and larger they looked forward to the birth of the baby. In fact, Blondie gave birth to two seven-month babies, a pair of gorgeous Japanese-looking twins! For the children, it provided a joyful diversion from their dull camp life and everyone celebrated the birth of Blondie's twins. The children fussed over them and were a great support for their mother, helping her to look after her two small babies.

THE MOTHERS of all the abused girls were very anxious about our health from the moment we were returned to them in Bogor Camp. Now they demanded that a gynaecologist be sent to our camp who could examine us at regular intervals, in case we had caught a venereal disease. And so a doctor from one of the nearby men's P.O.W. camps arrived at Kramat one day.

Dr Smith was a very nice man and very understanding. Equipment arrived at Kramat and Dr Smith set up his consulting room. The mothers were all very pleased and so were the girls, all except myself. As far as I was concerned, the arrival of the gynaecologist started the humiliations all over again.

At first I flatly refused to see the doctor and it

took a lot of persuasion from my mother to get me to go. How could I explain to her that every time I had to see him it was like being raped all over again? How would anyone understand that every time I visited him I was taken back to the Japanese doctor, who had raped me each time he visited the brothel? These experiences left me with a great fear of doctors.

Conditions in Kramat gradually got worse. As food became more and more scarce, we experienced real hunger pains. Rats were rampant and in the end we even ate them too. We also caught large black snails but they caused a throat disease and so we had to stop eating them. Dysentery was the biggest killer. The camp grounds were perpetually covered with sewerage overflow.

By this time my mother was in very poor health. She was skin over bones. She was so thin that I could lift her up as if she were a child. And then she caught pneumonia from sleeping on a damp mattress in a damp room, the walls of which dripped continually. She became so ill that she was moved into a make-shift hospital for the dying. Delirious, she didn't know anybody but me and would only take food from my hand. My sisters and I went without our rations so as to give the food to our mother.

Medicine, pills and tablets were the most sought after and precious possessions in the prison camp. Everyone tried to hang onto them in case they were needed to save someone's life.

When Yvonne, one of the volunteers from the

Semarang brothel, heard that mother was so very ill, she came to see me and handed over her last pills and tablets.

'I always liked your mother', she said. 'Perhaps these can help.'

I can't remember exactly what she gave me, but one tube, at least, contained vitamin pills. Dear Yvonne, she always did have a heart of gold.

My heart ached to see my mother lying so small, so helpless in the room for the dying. But I was determined that she was not going to die. I put my trust in God and got all my friends to pray for her. I got word through to the nuns in the main part of the camp and as I squatted in the mud, with my ear pressed close to the fence, I heard one of them speak.

'My dear Jan,' she said, 'never give up hope. We will all storm heaven with prayers for your mother.'

We prayed novenas, we prayed rosaries and litanies and my mother did not die.

Be full of courage

THERE WERE periodic rumours spread around the camp that the war was nearly over. It was 18 January 1945, and my twenty-second birthday. Fien and Céleste had managed to create something that looked like a birthday cake out of saved-up rations. My hair was back to normal again and because it was my birthday I decided to put on my one good dress.

All the women had saved one dress for when the war was over, so that they would look beautiful when meeting their husbands again.

It was not long after this that we saw a plane one morning, flying quite low over our camp. We screamed and jumped with excitement when we realised that it was not a Japanese one. From the plane dropped leaflets, like manna from heaven! They were scattered everywhere and we rushed to grab them and find out what they said.

'Be full of courage and perseverance', we read. 'The war will be finished soon.'

The leaflets were immediately destroyed but a Dutch friend of mine in Adelaide still has one of these messages from the Allies. The Japanese ordered us to hand in the leaflets immediately, but my friend managed to hide her piece of paper, carrying this amazing good news.

The leaflets did wonders for the morale of the women but they did not stop them from dying. Death was still all around, with women and children dying every day, especially the very young and the elderly. My sister, Céleste, was still wearing the same clothes that she had when she came into the camp. Because of the lack of food, she had virtually stopped growing.

Hiroshima was bombed on 6 August 1945. For us in Java, the war ended on 15 August of that year with the unconditional surrender of Japan's armed forces. It was at that time that planes again came flying over our prison camp. They were not Japanese

119

planes, as we at first thought, but allied planes and what excitement there was when we realised it!

The planes dropped food, lots and lots of biscuits and medicine, including penicillin, which had only recently been discovered. It saved my mother's life, my mother lived!

The food was distributed and my sisters and I sat down to our first 'freedom dinner', as we called it. We ate so much rice on that first day that it gave us terrible belly ache. Our stomachs had shrunk over the years and could not hold the large amount of food. We soon learned our lesson and from then on took it easy and did not eat too much all at once.

THE MOMENT we realised that the war was really over, someone in our camp produced a Dutch flag out of nowhere. None of us knew where it had come from but it sent shivers down our spines and we were all in tears as we saw the beloved red, white and blue flag hoisted in the air after three and a half years of occupation.

There was great confusion in the camp as everyone tried to find out if relatives had survived, and the Red Cross did a tremendous job. But we still had to spend the next five months in Kramat because we had nowhere else to go. In the meantime, food was delivered and doctors arrived to tend to the sick. The most seriously ill, including my mother, were transported to an outside hospital. She looked so pale, so little, so old and fragile as she was carried away from us. Once again we were separated and I was left to take care of my two younger sisters.

Gradually news from the outside world reached us and with it came news of husbands and fathers. God had been good to us. My whole family had survived the war, including my father, who had been imprisoned by the Japanese on Sumatra, and my elder brother, Ward, who had been a prisoner of the Germans in Europe. My grandfather, Henri, had survived the war and so had Aline.

WHEN WE were reunited in Holland in 1946 my father finally told me his story. It was one evening when we were alone together, our first opportunity to really talk to each other. He had suffered the most traumatic experiences at the hands of the Japanese, the memories of which haunted him for the rest of his life.

Every year, during the month of September, he relived the horrifying details of the sinking of the *Junyo Maru*, crying like a child. He had been in military service when the Japanese troops landed in Java on 1 March 1942. After the Dutch army capitulated, he was interned in a Japanese prisoner of war camp in Tjimahi and later in Makassar Camp, on the outskirts of Batavia, or Jakarta.

In September 1944, the inmates of Makassar Camp, including my father, were taken in trucks to Tandjong Priok, Batavia's harbour. From here, thousands of prisoners of war were transported to work on the so called 'death railroads' in Burma and Sumatra.

On arrival at the docks, my father's heart sank as he saw the *Junyo Maru*, a rusty old Japanese cargo ship. The first to go on board were the four thousand Javanese coolies, who had been forced out of the 'kampongs', or villages, to join the 'romusha', meaning soldiers.

On 16 September, around midday, the *Junyo Maru* left the harbour for Padang, Sumatra, making its way through the Soenda Strait. Six and a half thousand people were crammed on board, including two thousand five hundred prisoners of war.

The men were crammed in like sardines. If one had to relieve oneself, it often had to be done on the spot, causing a nauseating smell. In addition, the sea voyage was a very dangerous one because the waters were full of allied submarines.

On Monday afternoon, 18 September 1944, the *Junyo Maru* was hit by a torpedo, which tore open the hull of the ship. Hell broke loose as the four thousand 'romushas' panicked and tried to make their way onto the upper deck. Shortly after, a second torpedo hit the back of the ship and it began to sink. My father found himself down below, near the engine room, and he had to fight his way through to the top deck. He kept his wits and immediately took off his shoes, socks and clothing until he stood in his underpants. He even tossed out his beloved rosary beads.

Among the panic-stricken crowd, he caught sight of Father Xavier Vloet, the Carmelite army chaplain.

'Get ready to jump overboard', he shouted at Father Vloet.

'My task is to remain here on board where the men still need me', said Father Vloet, shaking his head. 'In any case, I can't swim.'

My father handed him something that might act as a life buoy and begged him to jump. But Father Vloet refused. He stayed at his post, fulfilling his duty as a priest, blessing the men and giving them all a general absolution. He made the sign of the cross on my father's forehead, then they embraced and my father made the terrifying jump into the cold ocean waters. Father Vloet was one of the twelve hundred and seventy-eight Dutch prisoners of war who perished during the sinking of the *Junyo Maru*.

Being a strong swimmer, my father's first thought was to swim as far away as possible, so he would not be sucked under by the force of the sinking ship. Looking around he found a plank of wood and grabbed it as a God-send. A little later he spotted another piece of wood and an army knapsack, with rope, floating on the water. With the planks and the rope, he managed to make something to hang on to. Six other men came to his aid and together they were able to make a small raft, just big enough to hold them afloat. All around them there were men crying for help and drowning.

The Japanese had taken possession of the life boats on the ship and any drowning victim who tried to hang on to their life boats had his hands cut off. A very real dilemma faced my father when one of the Javanese tried to get on to their small raft, nearly causing it to capsize. The man begged to be taken on board but with so many others also trying to get on he had to be refused. It would have meant that all seven of them already aboard would sink with him.

My father told the man to grab a plank of wood to make his own raft, but the man was obviously too tired to do so.

'Do you believe in God?' my father asked him. 'Then ask God to forgive you all your sins.'

He baptised the drowning man and then he had to loosen the hands that grabbed the raft. Slowly, before his eyes, the man disappeared into the deep waters.

This incident left a deep scar on my father's soul, causing him many sleepless nights and night-mares.

'I had no choice', he sobbed bitterly when he told me the story.

For two days and two nights they drifted on the ocean sea, then they were picked up by a Japanese patrol boat which was searching for survivors. Together with thirty other survivors he was taken to the death camp of Pakan Baroe in Sumatra. There he was forced to work on building the 230-

kilometre railroad, cutting through the dense jungles of Sumatra.

Many prisoners of war died from dysentery, malnutrition, malaria, exhaustion and tropical ulcers. Some just fell to their death. My father survived. He suffered intensely in the Pakan Baroe camp and his body was scarred with the marks of severe beatings and torture. The Japanese might have broken his body but they were never able to break his spirit.

Lily Kraus

WHEN THE war had been ravaging Europe, a great number of artists had turned to the Netherlands East Indies to perform there. The famous pianist, Lily Kraus, was one of these and was on tour in Java when the Japanese invasion took place in 1942. She, too, had been interned in Kramat prison camp. Now, after three and a half years, Lily Kraus was desperate to touch the keyboard again.

A piano was found for her and brought into the camp. She was delighted, and for the following months the strains of Chopin, Listz and Schumann could be heard. They had never before sounded so sweet and even Lily's endless scales were music to our ears.

Now that the war had ended and the gates opened, there was no longer a division in Kramat and we were able to mix freely with women from the other part of the camp. I was eager to meet the nuns as I had never been able to talk to them face to face. As I made my way through the camp I asked one of the women for directions. She turned rudely away from me and I heard some other women whispering, 'Look, there goes one from the whore camp'. It made me feel so ashamed and so I suffered more humiliation and the silence continued.

What was the use of trying to explain? Nobody believed us. Even my young sisters suffered insults because of what had happened to me. The dear nuns, however, received me with open arms. It amazed me how, through all the war years, they had managed to wear their habits, even though these did not look so white any more.

The nuns gave me the good news that a Catholic priest was coming to our camp that Sunday and that he would offer mass for us. My heart was overjoyed! After all this time I would be able to celebrate mass again and receive Holy Communion.

I felt a desperate need at this stage to talk to a priest and after mass I arranged to meet him, wishing that I could have seen dear Father Diderich instead of a priest I did not know. Feeling rather shy, I sat down to talk to him, telling him the story of my ordeal at the hands of the Japanese.

It was painful and difficult for me and at times I had to pause and swallow my tears. The priest sat motionless throughout my story. Finally I told him that I still wanted to be a nun and asked him for guidance and advice. There was a deadly silence. Nervously I began to bite my lower lip and wriggle my fingers. When his response finally came, my heart sank. I still remember what he said, word for word.

'My dear child', he replied, 'under the circumstances and because of what has happened to you, I think it is better that you do not become a nun'.

Looking back I realise that the advice he gave me was totally wrong and unnecessarily cruel. I was shattered and sadly disappointed by what I had been told. It gave me a terrible inferiority complex. Was I not good enough now to embrace the religious life? Had I suddenly changed? Was I soiled and dirty?

I had come for understanding and support and instead I walked away totally confused, neglected, unwanted and unloved. I had always regarded the words of a priest as absolute, so I did not question his opinion. It meant I had to come to terms with the fact that the convent was not the place for me. But Christ, too, had been scorned, rejected and misunderstood and this gave me courage. As always, my faith remained as strong as ever.

WITH MY mother in hospital I was responsible for the welfare of my sisters, who were now fourteen and eleven years old. Three and a half years of their precious childhood had been wasted away in prison camp.

The war was over but for us women in Kramat

Camp, Batavia, more terror still lay ahead. In the months following the Japanese surrender, the Indonesian independence movement waged war against the Dutch. The Indonesians did not want to return to Dutch rule and, spurred on by the Japanese anti-Dutch propaganda, they turned against us with violence.

In the camps we were easy targets for Indonesian terrorist attacks. These took place mainly at night, when terrorists jumped over fences into our compound, wielding knives and hand grenades. It was horrifying to see women and children killed so brutally after surviving three and a half years at the hands of the Japanese.

One of my best friends from the Ambarawa Camp, who was also forced into one of the Semarang brothels, was killed by a knife attack as she crouched beside me on the floor. It was a miracle that I wasn't killed as well. The attacker had jumped through a window and landed on top of her, slashing her with his knife.

Fifty years later I visited the war cemetery for the women and children who had died in the camps and I was able to lay a small bouquet of flowers at the grave of this brave girl.

During these five months it was very dangerous for us to leave the camp. We were told that if we did so it would be at our own risk. However, I resolved to continue to visit my mother in the hospital, a twenty-minute walk each way. Every time I made this walk I faced possible death at the hands of the snipers but I had faced death so many times already that it didn't seem to matter any more.

I recall one day in particular when I saw an Indonesian man perched in a tree above me, armed with a knife. I pretended not to see him and with my heart pounding in my chest, I kept on walking. Arriving at the hospital was traumatic for there were always Dutch casualties being brought in — people covered in blood who had been knifed, cut up or shot by the Indonesians. The situation had become so dangerous that British troops of the 23rd Indian Division were sent to the Dutch East Indies. These soldiers, previously stationed at Singapore, had just been through the Burma campaign and were en route to England. Instead of going home they were diverted to Java to protect us.

There was great jubilation at the arrival of the British troops, which included not only British military but also an Indian division of Ghurka soldiers. Machine guns were positioned at every corner of the camp and constant watch was maintained by fierce-looking Gurkhas. For the first time in nearly four years I felt safe again!

The arrival of the British troops brought great joy to our camp. The soldiers shared their army rations with us. Imagine opening a can of peaches! It tasted like nectar from the gods! The children were given chocolates. Some little ones had never even seen a bar of chocolate before.

Dances and parties for the women and children were organised. The children laughed again and the women once more took pride in their appearance. Indeed the British did not only save our lives, they were most generous and good towards us. For this they have never really been fully acknowledged.

It was with the arrival of the British troops that I met Tom Ruff. I was passing through the front gate of the camp on one of my visits to my mother. A handsome soldier approached me, telling me that it was too dangerous to leave the camp without an escort.

'Tell me where you want to go and I will take you in my jeep', he said.

From then on Tom took it upon himself to make sure I reached the hospital safely each time I wanted to visit my mother. With a co-driver at his side, whose rifle was pointed, ready to shoot, Tom would drive at high speed through a rain of bullets, while I crouched on the floor in the back of the army jeep. This was the beginning of a wartime romance and Tom and I began to meet regularly.

THE YOUNG girls in particular but indeed all the women enjoyed the dances and the parties that the British organised for us at their quarters, a former Dutch high school in Batavia. I had two decent looking dresses left and I used to ask Tom, before going to a dance, 'Shall I put on the blue dress or the white dress?'.

I began to get very fond of him and so did Fien and Céleste, perhaps because he used to give them his ration of chocolates. Tom was kind and gentle, uncomplicated, and in one word, a 'good' man. When I realised we were falling in love I decided to tell him my story.

We were sitting in the jeep, just the two of us when I told him of my wartime experiences at the savage hands of the Japanese. I could see the tears in his eyes as he let me tell my story without interrupting me. Knowing what had happened to me did not make the slightest difference to Tom or to his love for me. Unlike the Catholic priest who had so wrongly judged my situation, Tom responded with love and understanding and my self-esteem and confidence began to return.

He thought it was important to report this Japanese war crime, so he took me to the highest military authority at the British Army Police Headquarters. I told them my story but never heard any more about it.

Tom and I had only known each other a couple of months when we decided to become engaged. It was a Christmas Day party in 1945 and an Indonesian band played 'I'll be loving you always'. Tom produced a green jade engagement ring and slipped it on my finger.

SOON AFTER, we were reunited with my father and left for Holland on one of the Dutch ships. During the six-month period between returning to Holland and our marriage, Tom and I wrote to each other every day.

You can say a lot more in letters than you can say face to face and I think through these letters, Tom realized that it was hard for me to face the sexual part of married life and that he would have to be very patient with me. Finally, with this kind and gentle man, I prepared to leave my wartime memories behind and to start a new life for myself in England.

I took the night boat from the Hook of Holland and was met at Harwich by Tom and his parents. I was terribly excited and yet scared at the same time. It was the first time I had seen him without his uniform and I hardly recognized him. He looked so different in his rust-coloured sports coat.

We were married on 14 August 1946, and lived in a house that I called 'Zonnehoek', meaning 'Sunny Corner'.

I wanted to start a family straight away but because of all the damage that had been done to my body I was not able to carry a pregnancy through. In fact I had three miscarriages before I was operated on and had major surgery done. Eventually, I had two daughters, Eileen and Carol.

We lived in England for fourteen years and they were very happy and wonderful ones. In 1960, we migrated to Australia and I have never regretted the move. Australia has been good to me and I love my new country. We have been happy here.

Part 4

Breaking the Silence.

OVER THE years there had been many moments when I was on the point of telling my daughters the truth. I remember sitting with Carol, watching an Anzac Day march in the early 1980s. A group of feminists had joined the march, 'disrupting' the usual male-dominated proceedings.

These women were angry. They wanted justice and acknowledgement for women who had been raped in war. As they were forcibly removed from the march, I was crying out inwardly, 'They're right! It's true. If only people knew!'

I felt as though I had spent my whole life waiting for the right time to tell my daughters. But I had hidden my secret so well, there were hardly any clues.

How could my daughters have known the reason why I always said on birthdays or special occasions, 'Whatever you do, don't buy me flowers!'.

How could they know that flowers were forever associated in my mind with that horrendous first night in the brothel, and with my flower name, pinned up on the notice board at 'The House of the Seven Seas'.

Sometimes, if I was unwell, my girls would say, 'Mum, why don't you go to the doctor?'.

'I'm as strong as an ox,' I would reply, 'and I *don't* need a doctor!'.

How could they understand?

From time to time, my daughter, Eileen used to ask me, 'Why are you staring into space like that Mum?'.

'I'm only thinking', I would reply. There was no way I could have told her then.

Another incident that stands out in memory. I was at Bondi Beach with Carol and her little daughter. At two years old, Ruby was the typical European cherub, with a mass of golden curls and blue eyes.

We were pushing the pram along the promenade when the usual busload of elderly Japanese tourists climbed down from their coach, armed with their expensive cameras and videos. Looking at them, I realized that many of the men were old enough to have been soldiers during the war.

One of them approached me, gesturing that he would like to hold Ruby for a photograph. My overwhelming instinct was to grab her and flee but instead, I found myself smiling politely and obliging him. Carol noticed something wrong.

'Anything the matter Mum?'

I smiled, shaking my head. Here again was another lost opportunity.

Living with the secret of what had happened to me was an enormous burden. Nobody can imagine what it means to have something within yourself so terrible that you'd love to talk about it to other people, but you cannot, because you feel this terrible shame.

Nobody must know, and you carry the burden

135

all your life and you're always afraid that somehow, sometime, it's going to come out.

For fifty years I had wanted to scream it out but for obvious reasons, I could never do this. I could never talk about it, not even with my own family. Nor could the other women.

FIFTY YEARS of nightmares, of sleepless nights. Fifty years of pain that could never go away, horrific memories embedded in the mind, always there to be triggered off.

All through the early part of 1992 I had been moved to tears each time I saw the plight of the Korean 'comfort women' on television. I watched them with pain in my heart as they were sobbing for justice. All I wanted to do was to put my arms around them and hug them. I should be with them, were my thoughts.

That's when it really started. I had this strong feeling inside me. I've got to be with those women. I've got to back them up. And suddenly, I felt that the story I had carried for all those years, in my heart, could now be told. The courage of those Korean women gave me courage. At long last it could be told.

And how dare the Japanese call these poor abused women 'comfort women', I thought, as I watched them on the television. The euphemism 'comfort women' is an insult and I felt it was a pity that the media were also continually using these words. We were never 'comfort women'. Comfort means something warm and soft, safe and friendly. It means tenderness. We were war-rape victims, enslaved and conscripted by the Japanese Imperial Army.

THE FIRST Korean so-called 'comfort woman' to speak out was Mrs Kim Hak Sun. After all her family had died, and no longer feeling ashamed, she decided to demand compensation from the Japanese Government. Because of her courageous example, other 'comfort women' came forward and joined her in legal action against Japan.

Up to that time the Japanese government had not even apologised to the 'comfort women'. They had shown a total indifference to the problem and even denied the fact that Japan had forced thousands of women into prostitution in brothels for the Japanese army. I could see that the Asian 'comfort women' needed the support of European women. This had happened to Dutch girls too. Rape in war must be recognised as a war crime. Perhaps when a European woman came forward, Japan would take notice.

The war in Bosnia was showing me that the world had not changed. Women were again being raped as if it were a natural consequence of war, as if war could make it right. It was always played down.

'Men are like that. That's what happens in war. They must have encouraged it.'

I could see that this was not something that only happened fifty years ago. I had to tell my story, feeling that it might help to stop these atrocities from continuing.

It was with these feelings building in me that I decided to lay a wreath at the Adelaide War Memorial to commemorate the fiftieth anniversary of the surrender of Java to Japanese troops. It was a Sunday, 8 March 1992.

Through the local *Messenger Press* and the Adelaide *Advertiser*, I had invited people to join me for this occasion, especially those who had been in Japanese prison camps in Java during the Second World War. I had also invited the Japanese people to stand beside me as a sign of peace and reconciliation. That day I felt no anger, no bitterness, no hatred against the Japanese people. Only in forgiveness can healing be found.

As I laid my wreath that morning the faces of the women and children who had been in prison camp with me came vividly to mind. These women endured many horrors, insults, brutalities, rape and starvation in appalling conditions. Today, I wanted to pay tribute to their courage, their suffering and their endurance, and commemorate the thousands of women and children who died in Japanese camps. I saw again many of the faces of these brave women, their stories unknown to the world. They did not return from war like heroes, wearing their medals. They came back wearing their scars.

I looked at my wreath as it lay there at the steps of the war memorial. It was somehow urging me to tell the other story, the one story that had still to be told; the shameful story of one of the worst human rights abuses to come out of the Second World War. I knew that now, after fifty years, I wanted to tell it, but how and when I did not know.

When I laid my wreath that Sunday, it was my tribute to all the brave women that no one knew about, women who had suffered as I did at the brutal hands of the Japanese.

IT WAS late that year, October 1992, that I received a letter from Do Huisman in Holland. Do knew of my war-time experiences. 'Dear Jannie, I am writing on behalf of the Foundation of Japanese Honorary Debts. I'm asking if you'd be willing to be a witness ...'

She was looking for someone to speak at an International Public Hearing in Tokyo concerning Japanese war crimes and post-war compensation. I knew then that here was my opportunity to speak out.

The hearing was to take place in Tokyo, from 9-10 December 1992, and was supported by the Japan Federation of Bar Associations, and by Tokyo-based, human rights citizens groups.

I wanted to be that witness, but for me that meant telling my daughters, my grandchildren, my family, friends and fellow parishioners, the story that I had kept silent in my heart for almost fifty years. This was still the hardest decision for me to make.

How does a mother tell her daughters, a grandmother tell her grandchildren, that she was systematically raped and beaten daily for three months by the Japanese military during the Second World War?

I decided that the way to tell my daughters of my terrible secret was to write the story down in a notebook, and in this way they could read it quietly by themselves. Perhaps this was the easy way out but I still felt so much shame. I was not yet ready to tell them the story face to face.

One September morning, I took a taxi to Adelaide airport where I was to meet my youngest daughter, Carol. She was en route to Alice Springs to do some paintings in central Australia for her next exhibition. At the airport I was to pick up Ruby, now a little girl of five, to look after her while Carol was away.

It was only a short stop-over and as always we had so much to say to each other. I felt terribly nervous and I could feel the notebook burning in my bag.

'This is it,' I thought, 'there's no turning back now.'

It was about the most important moment in my life. As soon as I handed over the notebook, my darkest, innermost secret would be out. As the call came for Carol to board the plane, I slipped the notebook in her hand luggage.

'Here, read this', I said simply.

She looked at me curiously and we kissed and hugged and waved goodbye. I was crying when I took my little granddaughter by the hand to return home with me.

When Carol read my story on the plane, she was completely devastated. She burst into tears and could not stop crying. The passengers sitting near her could see how distressed she was and did not know what to do. The air hostess kept giving her boxes of tissues. Everyone thought that perhaps a close relative had died.

I gave Eileen, my elder daughter, her copy of the notebook the next day, so that she could read it quietly at home. She came to me when she had read it and put her arms around me, unable to speak. My daughters cried for weeks on end, devastated that something so horrific could have happened to their mother and feeling that it would take them a long time to come to terms with it.

Japan

WHEN I told Carol that I was going to Tokyo to give evidence at a hearing, she was both impressed and shocked.

'Mum, you can't possibly go to Japan by yourself!', she said. 'We're coming with you.'

I had not told any of my friends in the parish that I was going. Somehow, I still had the naive idea that I could slip away for a week without anybody missing me.

We travelled with Japan Air Lines and as soon as I heard a male Japanese voice coming through the sound system, my whole body shuddered. That fear was still with me as strong as ever. Carol noticed it. She squeezed my hand.

'Mum, you will have to get used to that sound', she said. 'You will soon be surrounded by Japanese.'

As I watched Australia disappearing from the satellite map on the video screen, and Japan slowly coming closer, I knew that soon I would be entering a totally Japanese world. I was terrified.

WE ARRIVED in Tokyo on 6 December. The two-hour journey into the city on a crowded train was nightmarish. We arrived at our hotel, late and exhausted. The hotel restaurant was closed and we found ourselves walking the back streets of the old part of Tokyo. Finally we found a small restaurant.

In our party were Carol, her husband, Ned, myself and two representatives from the Dutch 'Foundation of Japanese Honorary Debts'. They were the American lawyer, Russell Huntley, and the Dutch lawyer, Gerard Jungslager, himself a survivor of the prison camps. He was to be a guardian angel, at my side, throughout the Tokyo hearing. I sat next to Carol, studying the menu.

Looking up I saw the proprietor, a fat, sleazy-looking Japanese man, leaning against the kitchen door post, eyeing me up and down with that same look that I remembered so well from the brothel. It plunged me back into that dark past and I almost panicked, feeling the fear coming up my body. It sent shivers down my back. I froze.

Carol had noticed the man too and the way he was looking at me.

'Come on Mum, let's get out of here', she said, sensing my reaction.

It brought home to me once more the deep scar that was left on my body. There was still so much healing to be done, even after all these years.

THE EVENING before the International Public Hearing, a reception was organised for all the participants. There, in that hot and crowded room, I finally met some of the Asian 'comfort women'. I was to give testimony alongside these brave women the following day.

We couldn't speak to each other. We had no common language but I couldn't wait to put my arms around them. I noticed one woman in particular. She was Chinese and dressed all in black — long black pants with a black Chinese top. She looked so frail and small. Her face wore the lines of long suffering but her eyes still held a fighting spirit.

I went across to meet her and as we embraced, it seemed as if my whole life of suffering suddenly dissolved in the arms of this tiny woman. We held each other for a long precious moment.

That evening I met many wonderful Japanese people. I was showered with gifts and expressions of sympathy and support. It seemed as if this younger generation of Japanese people wanted to make up for the sins of their fathers. I soon realised that the week in Tokyo was going to be extremely emotional, but that it would be rewarding and healing too.

The International Public Hearing was to take place the following day, 9 December 1992, at the Kanda Panse, Tokyo. Before the hearing I was asked to do a television interview for a prime-time current affairs show.

I looked into the eyes of the young Japanese interviewer as I told my story publicly for the first time. As I watched the tears roll down her cheeks, I realized that there was a new generation of young Japanese people who wanted to know the truth.

From 2p.m. to 8p.m. that day, witnesses from the former so-called 'comfort women' of Korea, Taiwan, the Philippines, China, and myself, from the Netherlands East Indies, gave testimony. As well, victims of forced labour — men from China, Korea, and Sakhalin — told their stories of unspeakable suffering. The auditorium was packed. There was a zoo of reporters and cameramen from all over the world.

I listened intently, filled with emotion, to the first three women as they told their stories of indescribable humiliation, torture, suffering and persecution. Many in the audience cried. The third testimony came from a Chinese woman. As she told her story of the barbarous crimes inflicted upon her by the Japanese military she was so overcome by the memories that she fell backwards and passed out on the podium.

The red curtains were hastily drawn together and a doctor materialised. The auditorium was in an uproar and I was the next speaker. To my surprise, I was not nervous. I made a conscious effort to appear calm and composed as I moved to the centre stage to reveal to the world my haunting secret.

With Carol and Gerard on either side of me, I sat at the table to give my testimony. As part of the statement, I made the comment that I had forgiven the Japanese for what they had done to me but I could never forget. Later that day, one of the Japanese human rights lawyers approached me.

'I cannot understand,' he said, 'why do you want to forgive?'

He did not think that it would advance our cause.

Ned had been out in the auditorium with all the journalists, video-taping my testimony. When I had finished speaking, there was a stampede, as journalists and cameramen rushed out to get the story to their editors.

The South Korean women were due to speak next. They were over twenty in number, all dressed in white, their traditional colour of mourning. One of them rose to give testimony.

She was followed by a woman from North Korea, similarly dressed, but in beige. Her story of torture and suffering was particularly heartbreaking. While she was speaking, the group of women from South Korea were so moved that they began to gravitate slowly towards the stage. They crept closer and closer and finally, unable to restrain themselves any longer, they mounted the stage and surrounded the woman, embracing her.

'We were in the north and we never knew the same thing was happening to our sisters in the south', the woman cried out.

North and South Korea might have been at loggerheads with each other, but here, on this stage, the women from North and South Korea embraced in solidarity, united by the same grief and anguish.

Still sobbing, the women were ushered from the stage. One of the South Korean remained for a moment.

'Why is it that Korean women have been subjected to such horrors?', she cried out, in pain. 'Why was the blossom of our youth ripped apart? ... And you ignored us!'

In the auditorium there was a fellow country-man from Australia, a young journalist from the Australian Broadcasting Corporation's '7.30 Report'.

For some time he had been putting together a report on the issue of the 'comfort women'. Directly after the hearing, he interviewed me. I asked him when it would go to air.

'Tomorrow', he replied.

I knew then that when I got off the plane in Adelaide all the people in my parish back home, all my friends, would know my story. How would they react?

Carol and I lay in bed in our hotel kimonos that night watching the TV session I had recorded earlier with the Japanese woman. They showed photographs of my family in Java — my mother, my father, my grandfather's beautiful home in Bandoengan.

It was the strangest feeling to see those dear people and that cherished past on Tokyo's biggest news current affairs program. These private moments had now become a part of history. I wept.

I could not sleep that night. My head, my heart were filled with a world of pain and suffering.

The following day, 10 December, the Symposium on war and human rights was held. It was during this symposium that Gerard handed me a fax — a Dutch newspaper clipping from that day. It was a front page story.

Ellen van der Ploeg, whom I had gone to high school with in Semarang, and who had also been put in a brothel by the Japanese, had come forward in the press and put her story next to mine.

I was so delighted and I told the good news to the people at the symposium.

'You know what's going to happen,' I said, 'I think they're all going to come forward now, and what a strength we will be!'.

It was then that I knew that I wanted to go back to Holland and find some of those girls again.

Many peace groups were present at the symposium. A group of women under the name 'Atomic Bomb Sufferers' — survivors of Hiroshima — came over to me during the interval of the meeting.

'Now we know that we were not the only people that suffered', they said, putting their arms around me.

A feeling of healing and peace came over me in the presence of these women. They gave me presents and postcards and I gave them handkerchiefs, printed with Australian wildflowers, which I had brought with me for such a purpose.

On the next day, 11 December, our group was received into the Diet, Japan's Parliament House. At the meeting in the Prime Minister's office, with Mr Sakutaro Tanino, Chief Cabinet Councillor for External Affairs, I was again given the opportunity to tell my story and express my concern. Mr Tanino was visibly moved and promised to pass on our message to his Prime Minister.

A wreath of forgiveness

FOR ME, the highlight of the week came at the end. I had not come to Japan with hatred and I wanted to show the Japanese people that I had forgiveness in my heart. With the help of Carol, I had made a 'Wreath of Forgiveness' out of Australian wildflowers, which we had carried with us, all the way from Australia. I decided to lay it at the 'Chidorigafuchi', the Memorial for the Unknown Soldier, which is situated in a beautiful quiet park.

At the public hearing, I had made a statement inviting people to join me at this ceremony and a diverse crowd had turned up at the Memorial site. These included the Dutch Ambassador to Tokyo and many human rights, peace and environmental groups. As well, there was a busload of former Japanese soldiers from the Second World War — a group working for world peace. I realized once more that for many of these men, the memory of their past crimes weighed heavily on them.

'These are ex-soldiers', said our interpreter, Keiko, 'determined never to fight again'.

They welcomed me with flowers, books and gifts and I was overcome with emotion as I shook hands with each one of them. It was, in a sense, the most confronting moment of my six day stay in Tokyo. Here I was, actually shaking hands with men who had served in the Japanese Imperial Army.

Before the laying of the wreath, I talked to all

these people, explaining the reason for my being here.

'Today, I am laying a wreath at your memorial in Tokyo, with the Japanese people, standing at my side. This wreath is a sign of peace and forgiveness. A sign of hope for the future of the world, the future of our children.

'I hope that after fifty years we have learnt the lesson, that we are putting the war behind us and that we can work together, towards a world of peace. A world without hatred and fear, without war and violence, but rather a world of peace and under-standing, friendship and love and freedom.'

Several elderly ex-soldiers and other peace-seeking men came forward to read out their prepared speeches and prayers. Some of these men were Christians and I was very touched by one man who gave a moving talk in broken English. He ended by praying that beautiful psalm, Psalm 51, with the words, 'My sin is always before me'.

Holding out my hands to the ex-soldiers, I concluded the wreath laying ceremony by praying the peace prayer of St Francis of Assisi. Keiko, whose father had been an officer in the Imperial Army, was deeply moved. As she translated my words, she started to cry and we concluded the speech together, holding hands. I could sense an intense oneness with these Japanese people, present here at this simple ceremony. The week in Japan was, for me, a continu-ally healing process.

No more secrets

WE FLEW out of Tokyo a week before Christmas. Leaving Carol and Ned in Sydney, I went on to Adelaide alone.

The first Monday morning after my return was my seventieth birthday. Carol had sent me a beautiful painting of my French grandfather, Henri, and his wife, Jeanne. As I got ready to go to the 8a.m. mass, there was a knock at the door. It was one of my close friends from the parish.

'Are you coming to mass, Jan?', she asked.

'Of course I am', I replied.

I showed her Carol's painting.

'Bring it with you,' she enthused, 'and we can hang it in front of the altar'.

I was surprised at her request but I took the painting along with me. We walked to the church, only a few minutes from my home, and I arrived at the door, expecting the usual modest turn-up of 'old faithfuls'.

The church was filled with people. All my friends had turned out. I heard voices all around me.

'Happy Birthday! ... Congratulations! ... Welcome back Jan!'

Flowers had been placed on the pew where I always sat.

One of the kiddies beamed up at me.

'Mrs Ruff, I saw you on TV!'

The parish was welcoming me back with open

arms. Father Cronin was offering up the mass for me. I was overwhelmed with joy and love for these good people.

I had feared the consequences of breaking the silence for so long. Since Do's letter, everything had happened so quickly and now, I had arrived home to peace, and love and acceptance.